Philip Walsh

VIEWS FROM THE BACK OF A TAXI

2007 EDITION

Illustrations by Mikl

Bloomington, IN Milton Keynes, UK

AuthorHouse™
1663 Liberty Drive, Suite 200
Bloomington, IN 47403
www.authorhouse.com
Phone: 1-800-839-8640

AuthorHouse™ UK Ltd.
500 Avebury Boulevard
Central Milton Keynes, MK9 2BE
www.authorhouse.co.uk
Phone: 08001974150

First published by AuthorHouse 3/27/2007

ISBN: 978-1-4259-8222-5 (sc)

A catalogue record for this book is available from the British Library

Typeset in Baskerville Old Face

Printed in Great Britain by Authorhouse

This book is printed on acid-free paper.

This book is dedicated to the memory of Alf Garnett, and his late lamented creator Johnny Speight, whose opinions on everything seem to make more sense with each day that goes by.

So, wake up and smell the coffee...

Contents

"How fortunate for leaders that men don't think."
ADOLF HITLER

Introduction

SOME of the most thought-provoking conversations I've ever had have been in the back of taxis.

It's not hard to see why. A taxi ride is like life: you know where you've come from and how you're going to end up, but you're not sure of the route, how long it's going to take or how you might get sidetracked along the way. Plus the fact that whilst you might like to think you're in charge of the trip, you're not actually in the driver's seat.

So, any conversation you can cram in is a bonus. Two people meeting for the first and probably the last time, knowing absolutely nothing about each other, with the chance to put the world to rights all in the space of an average taxi ride – what's that, twenty minutes? Long enough, I would say.

In total privacy you can have an uninhibited, relaxed, agenda-less exchange of views you won't get anywhere else. You're not going to lose your job because of something you've said. You can be indiscreet, offensive, arrogant and self-important, safe in the knowledge that there won't be any unpleasant consequences. And you better get to the point quickly. No time for wasted words, your destination is just around the next corner. This has great benefits. Without the time to beat about the bush, or couch your thoughts in 'politically-correct speak', it's amazing how clear things become. I remember appointing the next Conservative leader, sorting out old age pensions and ending the war in Iraq all between Fleet Street and High Street Kensington. What *are* these politicians doing?

Of course, the taxi driver has one hell of an advantage over you. He's a professional – and I don't mean just at driving. You might have a conversation like this once or twice a week, he'll have ten or twenty a day. Which must make him worth listening to. If only because his opinions represent the distillation, cross-fertilisation and general sorting of the thousands of views and conclusions his passengers have passed on to him. One minute a prominent politician, the next a businessman, a journalist, or a priest followed by a hairdresser. Zealots, fanatics, bigots, liberalists, obsessives, addicts, heteros and homos, men, women, blacks, whites, left-wing, right-wing, Christians, Muslims – they've all travelled in the back of his cab and he's put the world to rights with them all at some time or another. He's absorbed their common ground and their divides. And you get all that for the price of a taxi ride! Jeremy Paxman eat you heart out.

I started to write this book because it seemed to me that people who ought to know better were missing the point. Not just one point. Lots of points. Let's re-cap.

I was brought up in a world where we were taught to trust people. If somebody said he was an expert at something, you'd shut up, listen and learn. And then do as you're told. Now, fast-forward fifty years, and I'm fed up with being told what to do. More than that, I'm fed up with being told what to think. When I was a child I didn't mind and most of the time it worked. It's not that my Mum was cleverer than me, it's just that she'd been round the block a few more times. As a little boy I understood that, so I was happy to do as she said. Mostly, she was right. Right about not playing with the fire, not eating stuff I found at the bottom of the garden, right about wrapping up warm so as not to catch a cold. She was even right about my homework and not being horrid to girls. Later on Dad weighed in. He seemed to know things Mum didn't know, so now I had two people to listen to.

Then, one day it happened. As I moved into my teens, I began to see gaps in their knowledge. It hit me like a ton of bricks. Increasingly, their advice was inadequate, short of the mark - weird even. Why? Because we were getting into territories where they were out of their depth. This took me by surprise. If I couldn't rely on my parents to tell me what to do and think, whom could I rely on?

I tried others. To start with friends – male and female - relatives, older people, younger people, doctors, teachers, clergymen (not often), policeman and then, later on, accountants, lawyers, businessmen, financial advisers, even local politicians. All these people offering (and mostly charging) for their advice. Trouble is they hated it when I didn't take it. But, by then the truth was out.

Here it is:

Other people are usually wrong.

Think about it. How many people have you met who you wished you were like? How many of your knowledgeable, opinionated friends actually enjoy a lifestyle you envy? And where are all the millionaires? It must have struck you how few of those people who have an answer to everything have succeeded at the relatively simple task of making money - or, for that matter, anything else. Where is the evidence that others know better than you? I don't see it. I wish I did.

Therefore, it must stand to reason you can't rely on anyone. So, you'd better learn to rely on yourself. Listen to 'experts' by all means – they will certainly tell you the odd thing you didn't know – but make your own decisions. No-one else cares as much as you.

This is not a book about lifestyle or success. On their own those things don't matter. They're not projects. Nor is it a book about how to be happy, in my opinion one of the silliest and most misguided pursuits of our age.

So what is it? It's a book of opinions, thoughts - ideas, if you prefer. Some will say it is of no importance whatsoever, because the originators of these ideas are of no importance whatsoever. But then if experts are usually wrong, doesn't that mean that the opinions of the rest of us count even more? Doesn't it mean that my views, *your* views – not to mention the taxi driver's - are as important as anyone else's? In fact, isn't that exactly what so-called progress is supposed to be about? That our opinions *do* matter? I don't know how you feel, but to me it seems as if my views, your views, have never mattered less.

That's why I've put it all down on paper. Not because I want to influence anyone, not that I expect to make a difference, not even because it will make me feel better or earn me money But – and it's a big 'but' – if there's anything here that strikes a chord, rings a bell or you simply haven't heard said for a while, well, there's the thing.

These views have been assembled from countless journeys in the back of a taxi. The cabbie has been my sounding box and I his. They are the thoughts of predominantly ordinary folk and, as the late Dave Allen would have said, thank whoever your God is that there are still a lot of us around.

PHIL
2007

PS You might not be as lonely as you think.

Acknowledgement

IT is impossible to attribute the views and opinions expressed in these pages to anyone in particular, even if I had known or noted names, which, in the vast majority of cases, I didn't.

Often one conversation would lead to another at a later date. Sometimes I would deliberately set out to seek additional points-of-view. Then, when it came to writing it all down, my own thoughts and opinions inevitably intruded, sometimes in an effort to develop an argument, or merely in an attempt to shed some light where questions had remained unanswered. Occasionally, rage overtook reason. Sorry.

Still, I have tried to stay true to the spirit and robustness of those many exchanges and the passions they aroused at the time. Ninety per cent of taxi drivers work for themselves, which gives them a sharp perception of reality. They are known to suffer from high blood pressure, which I'd previously put down to stress and the sedentary job. Now, I think it is frustration: frustration with the human condition and our constant failure to learn from experience.

This book started life as an ill-assorted bundle of notes and reminders, mostly scribbled down hastily in waiting rooms and reception areas following some especially thought provoking ride with a highly articulate and opinionated man or, in one case, woman.

They may or may not recognise themselves in what follows but to all of them I express my thanks.

Democracy

I remember passing Downing Street once with a driver who got very hot under the collar about George Bush naively 'selling' democracy as the universal answer to everything. After all, we're the oldest democracy in the world and it's being stretched to breaking point here - witness the low turnout at elections. He told me he'd met at least two past Prime Ministers who shared this view. But he wouldn't tell me who they were.

WHY do some people find it so difficult to understand that democracy doesn't work everywhere?

It seems perfectly obvious that in order to succeed democracy relies on one thing - that after the vote, the losers agree to get behind and support the winners. Allow them to get on with the running of things. Bury the hatchet until next time around.

Naturally, because this is staring us in the face, we take it for granted. In reality it is a lot to ask. It's a sophisticated idea. Not everyone is gracious in defeat. In fact, it's a very English quality. Which is why it works here and only in a few other places where we've managed to export it.

So why should that be? It's because in this country the very differences that determine the opposing sides of the political argument are really very small indeed. After several centuries of living together, sharing common goals, traditions, beliefs, hopes and dreams, we are actually in agreement about nearly everything. In fact, we hugely exaggerate our differences. Take religion. Think of the fuss we've made about Catholics and Protestants. It's even led us to civil war. Ridiculous. On a world scale they are as good as identical.

It's because these differences are so minor that democracy works for us. Okay, we may pay a bit more tax under one party, or have a different approach to immigration under another – but we're not going to get slaughtered in our beds at night or have our children taken away from us. Or have the crimes of our great-grandparents avenged upon us. Not often, anyway.

We're lucky. We can have 60 million people in violent disagreement one day, with all the self-righteousness and dogma that goes with it, only for them all to unite behind someone who, twelve hours earlier, had incurred their acute dislike, even hatred. Or, at least, if not unite, agree to let them get on with governing the country for another five or ten years when the system will give us the opportunity to start all over again.

Now, compare this with elsewhere in the world. Places where people are so violently opposed to each other's views and culture that they couldn't possibly agree to be led by someone who just happens to have gathered the most slips of paper in a shoebox. Take any kind of tribal society. As far back as they can recall people have been at each other's throats. Tribal warfare has a long and honourable tradition, based upon the worship of rival gods, the animosity of one family towards another, the absolute requirement that each generation takes up the continuing fight against the foe.

Then someone comes along and says you've got to have an election and that whoever gets most votes will assume power. Why? This is precisely what your ancestors have conditioned you to prevent at all costs. And, anyway, it's all about numbers. A tribe doesn't forsake it's right to run its own affairs just because it's small.

So, what happens? The ballot takes place, someone gets elected and the voters who didn't get their own candidate immediately set about undermining the winner – often violently and with tragic consequences. The new leader, now vested with the full powers and accoutrements of elected office, in time will use this power to squash the opposition, now tagged 'terrorists', 'revolutionaries', 'enemies of the state' or 'insurgents'. But, of course, he never will. The more he hits back, the more they become convinced that they (their fathers, uncles and grandparents) were right all along. Protests become skirmishes, which, in turn, develop into mass murder and genocide.

And let's not fool ourselves into thinking these problems are all a long way away. They can happen on our doorstep and does. Look at Ireland, for a start. Then look only marginally further away to how the totalitarian Tito successfully kept the lid on Yugoslavia for nearly fifty years after the war. Then observe what happened when he died. The Chechens and Serbians were back at each other's throats within weeks. Sometimes dictatorship is the only way and if it's relatively benign, so much the better. But don't count on it. "Cometh the hour, cometh the man" works for monsters as well as heroes.

So let's not be naïve.

Democracy only works where there is a broad agreement already by the majority of people on most things. It can cope with the few small differences that remain.

What it can't do is resolve major differences between cultures, religions. It can't deal with historic divides. For countries like that we have to find – and tolerate – a different sort of system, which may sometimes be difficult for us to swallow. More often that will be our problem not theirs and it doesn't give us the right to interfere. In some cases it will be centuries before they are ready for some form of democracy.

If ever.

*It's only the powerful who have the choice
to relinquish power.*

Politicians

It's no surprise that cabbies don't have much time for politicians. They think most of them would fail abysmally in a proper job. Not long ago I was picked up by a driver who'd been reading about the Blairs' antics in the property market - "and these are the people running the country!" he chortled. What follows comes from dozens of similar exchanges.

OKAY, let's get them out of the way. It won't take long.

We'll give most of them the benefit of the doubt to the extent that they go into politics because they think there is an important job to be done ruling the rest of us and they'd be good at it. The best of them believe there's no point standing on the sidelines complaining; you might as well get onto the field of play where at least you stand the chance of affecting the course of events. Or not.

There's a number of problems with this. Let's take the analogy a bit further. Everyone who goes to a football match is an expert, but you wouldn't really want any of them on the pitch, would you? For the simple reason that the people actually playing the game are brilliant at it. They have huge natural talent to start with, they train hard and we pay them a fortune to do it. Yet, when it comes to politics we have no such demands nor expectations. In fact, quite the reverse. Merit and suitability for the job don't count. Nor does talent.

Just the ambition to get elected – plus the belief they know what's best for the rest of us and can't wait to give it a try.

In fact, just about the only similarity between politicians and footballers is they get paid precisely what they're worth. As in most fields of human resources, we get what we pay for. In the case of politicians that's about £60,000 a year - roughly what a middle manager would get in London if he was doing a proper job. Unfortunately, whilst we don't pay anything like enough to get top people into Parliament, it's sufficient for the middle-rankers to earn a living, pay the mortgage, take a nice family holiday and, in most cases, pay for their private medical insurance and the kids' education. So, not only do we have a system likely to attract mediocre people in the first place, once they're in they are going to hang onto to their jobs for dear life. After all, for most of them it's going to be the best job they're ever likely to have. There goes freedom of thought, independence of mind and conscience. No wonder they don't resign anymore. They can't afford to.

It wasn't always like this.

How have we arrived at this lamentable state of affairs? Well, we must not forget that like many other things in this country (I could ramble on about the Lawn Tennis Association, the MCC, the FA, local councils, hospital boards, etc, etc, etc) the system was invented when we still had a clearly defined class system. In those days the word 'amateur' meant something quite different. Today we regard amateurs as people who aren't good enough to earn their living at something. This wasn't always so. Not so long ago an amateur was someone who did a job without being paid for it. Full stop. He might be brilliant, but he didn't get paid. Why? *Because he didn't need the money.*

Now, this is difficult to get our minds round but, when I was a child, my father took me to cricket matches when Colin

Cowdrey (amateur), one of the greatest batsmen this country ever produced, batted at one end whilst Denis Compton (professional), equally brilliant, played at the other. No great difference in skill, ability or dedication, merely that one enjoyed amateur status, the other earned his living out of the game. The only time this mattered was when it came to choosing a captain. All else being equal, the amateur would get the job. Why? Because in those days it was considered the amateur could captain a team with only one thing in mind, namely, to do the job to the best of his ability, unselfishly, without having to worry about whether he could pay the household bills if he failed.

Somewhere along the line, 'amateur' and 'professional' started not to mix so easily and, at different times in different fields, they became separated. Nowadays, if you are spotted playing a sport well enough as an amateur, you expect to become a professional. It's a common ambition amongst young boys, and increasingly girls, to become professional sportsmen. Funny, but Denis Compton would have seen this the other way around – he would have loved to be able to play cricket just for fun of it. Only in a very few sports – golf, athletics and rugby, to name three – do amateurs and professionals still play side by side and even then not often. Not to mention complicating factors such as expenses, prize money and payments from the media.

It was the same in the military. The NCO and officer system of ranking came from the same idea that the people actually running the show would not get paid, they would do it out of a sense of honour and duty, but the troops would. And so on through vast swathes of our society, everything run by amateurs, overseeing the work of the professionals. Even today in many of our institutions, the professionals never get to run their own show – and politics is no exception.

Now, whatever you think about that way of doing things, the fact is we can't go back, nor, in fairness, would most of us want to. Charming though it may all seem, we simply don't have highly skilled, highly principled amateurs around anymore, or, if we do, not in sufficient numbers. What's more, we don't expect anyone to work for nothing. We feel more comfortable if they are being paid for their efforts. The trouble is we are at an in-between stage. If we want real professional expertise in any walk of life we have to pay a lot of money for it.

Here's the question: if we believe that the Chancellor of the Exchequer is a really important guy who effects all our lives, how can we justify paying him less than a quarter of Wayne Rooney's annual wage? Look at it another way - if we did pay senior politicians as much as footballers, how much higher would be the calibre of applicants for the job?

Right now, we are falling right down the middle and getting the worst of both worlds. Personally, I'm for expertise. I want brilliant people running our affairs, people with flair, talent, vision and imagination, not mediocre, interfering do-gooders with limited personal horizons, worries about their future and next to no experience of anything that really matters. I want to look up to our Prime Minister not because he is Prime Minister but because he inspires in me respect, admiration and a sense of how lucky we are to have him in the job.

These people do exist – not in large numbers, but then we don't need thousands of them. But the truth is that very few, if any, of them would ever choose to go into politics. And who can blame them.

There's also evidence that the genuinely politically motivated amongst us are finding more effective ways of expressing themselves by joining minority pressure groups and lobbying organisations.

So, I am not against paying politicians more money, quite the opposite. That's not to say the current crop deserve it but I'd like to think the next lot might.

Of course, there is another possibility; that politics and politicians don't really matter anymore. Truthfully, if it was not for the extraordinary and mutually self-serving pact between politicians and the media, we wouldn't know what they were doing most of the time anyway. Life would go on just the same for most of us.

Here's another thing. Have you any idea what your MP actually thinks? They should all have to write books like this.

By law.

"When London's Transport Commissioner is paid nearly ten times the Prime Minister the world has gone mad."

MP ALAN DUNCAN WHEN TOLD THAT AMERICAN
BOB KILEY IS PAID £1.1 MILLION A YEAR

Party Politics

'Who am I supposed to vote for when no-one represents my views?' is an all too familiar plea, quickly followed by: 'Frankly, I wouldn't give a toss for any of them!' Here's a different theory, putting the blame not so much on the politicians individually but the party system within which they have to operate.

ANY attempt at a democratic system needs an effective structure to enable it to work. In our case (and most other so-called democracies based on ours) this is a party system, each party representing the collective views of a large, recognisable chunk of the population. Here we run into a major problem, which at least accounts for the apparent irrelevance of politicians today. Namely, that the three parties we have – Labour, Conservative and Liberal – no longer represent the true divides in our society and, in truth, haven't for a long time.

Our present party structure came from a different era when these disparities were based on class, wealth and an acceptance of Christian values. These are not the issues of today. While the Conservatives still 'represent' the wealthy, managing, ruling class, and Labour the poor, downtrodden workers, for example, these categories within the population no longer exist to any meaningful degree. The huge expansion of the middle class after the war changed all that and our political parties failed to see that their traditional remits had become obsolete in the process.

While this was happening, a whole range of new divisions appeared so that we are now split into entirely different factions. Just list the real issues of today and you'll see where the true divisions lie: multi-culturalism, civil and human rights, federalism, regionalism, the environment, addiction and substance abuse, family life, the moral maze – as well as health, education, law and order and the economy. Apart from the last four, all of these issues fall beyond traditional party politics. So does the single most important issue of our time - the increasing invasion of the state into our private lives.

Is it surprising that politicians brush these tricky issues under the carpet, preferring to tread in more familiar, well-trodden territory?

Today's pressing problems, which we are failing to deal with, cut completely across old-fashioned political divides - and none of them have anything to do with 'bosses' and 'workers'. You'll find as much disagreement on any of these 'new' issues amongst conservatives as amongst socialists. Unless, of course, the party leaders call out the whips and make sure that no-one brings them up in the first place. Since the parties can't handle them, better not to talk about them at all. Which is precisely what has happened. The real issues that deeply concern people get swept aside - or sacrificed on the altar of political correctness - whilst politicians prattle on contentedly about the old party political chestnuts of yesteryear whilst the rest of us stand back and yawn.

In reality, of course, sensible politicians of all parties know this and are pretty much in agreement when it comes to the old issues anyway. As a result we have witnessed an unprecedented 'swapping' of policies, with New Labour stealing ideas from the Conservatives and vice versa, whilst the Liberals first had the centre ground swept from under them by New Labour and are now seeing what's left being filched by 'call-me-Dave'! Ideologies have become commodities, to be 'bought' and 'sold' by whatever party wants to tweak its appeal to the electorate on any given day. That's why seventeen million people couldn't be bothered to vote at the last election. (Bear in mind that Tony Blair was elected with less than ten million votes). That, plus the fact that no-one trusts our politicians anymore.

What can be done? Well, in the longer term, it must and will sort itself. If we continue to deprive ethnic minorities a hand in running the country (other than tokenism within the existing parties which is disgusting), eventually, they will find a voice of their own. Quite right. Others, opposed to a federal Europe, will come together as a focussed, cohesive group whilst those who believe that the future stability of a global society depends upon spiritual and moral issues, including the environment, will find a way of persuading the rest of us to take them seriously. A powerful force will emerge to resist the relentless march of state interference in our lives, to fight for the right of the individual to control his own destiny and to argue the case that government should serve and not dictate.

There will be others, too. By 'packaging' these ideas and building fresh political platforms, new parties will evolve; parties with whom we can identify and vote for, instead of feeling disenfranchised as we do now. Needless to say, for this to happen, we shall need to adopt some form of proportional representation, which is pretty normal in other multi-cultural societies - and, make no mistake, that is where we are heading. Not surprisingly, all three of our existing parties are opposed to PR. But then they would say that, wouldn't they?

How and when might all this come about? It's hard to say, but, with the present system imploding, it may not take so long. Politicians need to do what we elect them to do. They need to have vision, imagination – and lead.

If that means a wholesale re-structuring of the system within which they function, then so be it.

"Parliament is an assembly of one nation, with one interest, that of the whole...where not local purposes or prejudices ought to guide but the general good, resulting from the general reason of the whole."
EDMUND BURKE 1774

Human Rights

There's no doubt that the old Tony Martin case was a wake-up call. Every cabbie I've spoken to believes with a passion that Martin had every right to protect his property - with a shotgun if necessary - and that the burglars left any rights they may have had outside his front door when they decided to break in. This has led to some good exchanges on the subject of what 'rights' actually are and how we get them in the first place.

DEAR oh dear, what a muddle.

All very well intentioned, no doubt, but you can't help thinking that a new industry has emerged without anyone agreeing what its object was in the first place. That's not to say it didn't seem like a good idea at the time.

So, what to make of it? Let's start with the assumption that there is such a thing as a 'right'. If so, what is it and are we born with it? You know, that's difficult. We're born with opportunities, yes, but rights – not so sure. Let's see. For example, are we born with the right to have children,? Not necessarily, it would seem, since Nature routinely fails to equip some people to reproduce. Are we born with the right to be free? Not within Nature's gift apparently and, anyway, what does it mean? Are we born with the right to feed and clothe ourselves, to keep warm, to be educated, to be happy? Obviously not, if we are expecting Nature to provide all of this at the time of birth - two thirds of the world's population are born without any of them. So, if there are 'rights', it would appear to be beyond Nature to provide them. No, we're not born with them.

Are we talking, then, about something quite different? Are we saying that a right is something we bestow upon ourselves, man to man? In other words, that we are all entitled to have what we want, to be spoken to as we would like, to behave towards each other fairly, with courtesy, consideration and good will? And, if so, is this something that comes naturally?

It's interesting to take a child's perspective on this. I remember my daughters pleading "It's not fair!" at least a dozen times a day. Clearly children know what fairness is (perhaps that's something we *are* born with), but they pretty soon get used to the idea that there's not much of it about.

Of course, all of this was much easier when we had religion. Most of what we now call 'human rights' was in the Bible. So, although Nature may not have supplied us with rights in the first place, it was made pretty clear that God wanted us to treat each other kindly. "Love thy neighbour", although open to misinterpretation, must have seemed quite straightforward for a couple of thousand years. Strangely, though, it didn't go as far as preventing wars. Especially religious wars. Oh, and the Church didn't have much to say about homosexuals having the right to have children. Or, women having the right to be priests. It still doesn't, not that anyone is listening much anymore. So, maybe those things aren't rights after all.

Raincheck. If we're not born with rights, and they are just another way of describing human behaviour, then who decides what is a 'right' and what isn't?

Well, forgive me for not spotting it earlier - but of course, the answer is staring us in the face. We have a Court of

Human Rights, don't we? So, the answer to the 'Meaning of Life and Everything' isn't '42' as Douglas Adams told us after all. Actually, it is:

Lawyers

Quite a revelation, eh? As if we didn't know. And that includes all the lawyers who are working as politicians, too. It's lawyers who decide what 'rights' are and it's lawyers who grant them and take them away. On the face of it, that's great because the law works on the principle of argument. If you believe that you have a 'right', just go to the lawyers and they'll present the case for and against and, eventually, after a lot of people have made a great deal of money, a 'court' will tell you, once and for all, whether your particular 'right' is actually a 'right' or just something you want. Thereafter, thanks to the principle of precedent, once you've got it, so has everyone else.

This leads us on to another point; if 'rights' are defined and granted by humans to humans and not by some divine benefactor, are they permanent? In my opinion, rights can only ever be a moveable feast. If the men who terrorised the farmer Tony Martin had any 'rights' to start with, they gave them up the second they broke into his home. He shot one of them and went to prison. Wrong. Thank you, lawyers.

Now, I must declare that I don't have a lot of time for lawyers but I do know some very pleasant ones who are extremely intelligent. I don't know any who want to play God but, increasingly, we are asking them to do just that. In the process we have laid a minefield.

By it's very nature the law is a meddler. It works well enough most of the time at the relatively low level of sorting out people's day-to-day difficulties and bringing disputes to a conclusion. But it hasn't got a lot to do with right and wrong. I don't think the law has anything to contribute to the moral maze and history will bear out its impotence in matters of real importance. Where was the Court of Human Rights when Bush and Blair declared war on Iraq? What happened to the 'rights' of innocent Iraqis killed by American missiles? What about the rights of young soldiers who didn't want to get killed? Did they leave their right to live behind them when they went to war? You see what I mean. Rights that are invented by lawyers and politicians (most of whom are lawyers anyway) get shoved around to suit the convenience of the moment.

Foxhunting is a good example. For centuries the sort of people who hunt foxes were regarded as the paragons of our society, the upholders of the very fabric of the British way of life, including the legal system itself. Now, because someone has decided that foxes have rights, they are all criminals. Actually, they are the same people they were before, with the same values, the same attitudes and the same morals. It's the law that has changed, not them. No, we can't rely on the law and we shouldn't expect to. Some things can't be delegated and 'human rights' is one of them. This is an industry that should never have got started.

It's difficult to talk about 'human rights' without talking about politics and political correctness – another aberration of our age. It's easy to blame socialism with it's well-meaning but futile attempt to change human nature by introducing more and more legislation, rules and regulations. It can't be done. In the end all you do is create criminals out of people who simply don't share your point-of-view. Think how many of today's heroes were once regarded and treated as criminals – Nelson Mandela, to name one. Jesus Christ to name another. We can't rely on lawyers and politicians to get it even vaguely right.

No, so long as human rights are negotiable I can't take them seriously. As with so many other things in our flayling, formless society, when all else fails, all that's left is Common Sense and that is God-given in various measures to us all. The law failed Jesus Christ, Nelson Mandela, Tony Martin and the Iraqis. Common sense might not have done.

My common sense tells me that none of us are born with rights. Maybe we have the chance to earn some along the way, but that's an entirely different matter.

If you have never experienced the danger of battle or the loneliness of imprisonment, the pangs of starvation or the agony of torture, you are ahead of 500 million people in the world today

The Multi-Cultural Society

> *You can't ride through parts of London in a taxi*
> *without getting your ear bent on this one. In general,*
> *cab drivers aren't racist. Neither are they bigoted,*
> *anti-semitic, ageist or sexist. What they don't like is*
> *any kind of discrimination (probably because they see*
> *their fair share of it professionally) plus, to a man, they*
> *are - or were until recently - proud to be British.*

FIRST of all, let's emphasize that we are talking about 'multi-cultural' and not 'multi-racial'. So, before anyone shouts 'racist' (which they probably will anyway) this is not about whether people of different races can live happily together, it's about people with different cultures.

You might think the two things are the same, but they're not. In fact, I'd go so far as to say that the greater part of the problem stems from the fact that either accidentally - or sometimes quite deliberately - we get them confused.

Let's be clear on this. If everyone played the same game and abided by the same rules, it wouldn't matter what their race was. You could put a Chinese, an African, an Asian, an Arab and an Englishman in a room together and, providing they shared the same way of life, the same aspirations, values, beliefs, standards and ethics - and preferably the same history - they'd get on famously. Race wouldn't make a scrap of difference. But then, culturally, despite their origins, they'd all be the same.

For a multi-cultural society to work, however, these same people have to get on with each other knowing they will have major differences in all the above departments, starting with religion.

Just because religion is not the paramount force amongst the British that it once was, we make a fatal mistake if we underestimate its power in other cultures. In our predominantly humanist society, broadly speaking we try to sort out our problems through rational thought and debate. It has not always been so. Until relatively recently, should we defy the teachings of God, through Jesus Christ Our Lord, we did so at our peril. Folks would pray to God for guidance before making a decision of any importance. The Bible was our first point of reference, not the last. Once a course of action had been decided, action could be taken in the comforting knowledge that God had given it his seal of approval. Therefore, matters were out of our hands. We were merely the implementers of God's will.

Like it or not, we have evolved beyond that point. Or gone backwards, however you see it, it doesn't really matter. Either way, we don't do things that way anymore. The problem is that plenty of others do. And there are more of them than there are of us.

Let's take one fundamental difference that flows directly from this. Suicide bombers. In our culture if there is one thing we unanimously agree on, it's the need for self-preservation. What use are you to anybody dead? To many fundamental Muslims, however, the case for committing suicide according to the 'teachings' of their religion is blindingly obvious. In fact, under certain circumstances, it is positively heroic. These people are not idiots but their culture, in this case driven by faith, makes them appear to us to be nothing short of crazy. Now, if I lived next door to such a person, I am not saying that I couldn't get on with him on a day-to-day basis but, sooner or later, most probably in times of strife, these basic differences would emerge. We quite simply would not be able to understand each other. Don't tell me that we would somehow both be enriched by this experience, what is there to enrich? The fact is we disagree with each other profoundly and at the most basic level and, what's more, neither of us is going to change.

Religion can make life very difficult indeed. For centuries we have been obsessed with the differences between Catholics and Protestants, so much so it's led to wars. For heaven's sake, they're almost identical! Same God, same prophets, same texts, prayers, hymns, same beliefs. Just minor technical differences in the manner of worship. And contraception. Think of the trouble that's caused! Now we're trying to convince ourselves that people of totally different faiths can live contentedly, side by side! I don't think so.

You see, the vast majority of religious folk are evangelists. Sooner or later they'll try to convert you to their way of thinking. And, if you resist, or worse, show no interest, they can get very frustrated indeed. Where does frustration invariably lead? To violence.

It's not just religion. Customs, traditions, ancient rites, tribal rivalries, racism, sexism – all of these come into the equation. This is not easy.

For a long time we British thought that it would only be a matter of time before all these people realised how much better our culture was than theirs and then they would all change to our way of thinking. All we had to do was 'integrate' them into our society. Why on earth did we think that? We must be the worst at integrating in the world!

Try going to Marbella and seeing how well the British integrate. Do they want to learn the language, mix with the locals, eat local food, learn to dance flamenco and go to bullfights? Like hell they do. They live in little British communities, expect the Spaniards to speak English, start English/Irish pubs, make Spaniards cook fish and chips, hold English parties and watch Sky TV.

We even invented a word to describe it: "Ex-Pat" – the Englishman living temporarily away from home. Except most of them never came home. We behaved like this all over the world, from Shanghai to Bridgetown, Madras to Malaysia. So why on earth should we be surprised when folks from the Middle-East choose to congregate in Wembley and behave in exactly the same way?

It's not as if there is any universally agreed way to tackle the problem. The Americans say "You can't come here", the French say "You're welcome but don't expect us to treat you differently," and we say "Come here, set up your own cultures within ours and we'll move everything around to accommodate you." Result: the whole world hates the Americans, the French have got civil war and we've lost our heritage.

I've heard it said that this is adult stuff, that to see integration at work all you have to do is look in schools where children are blissfully unaware of cultural divides. Not in my experience, I'm afraid. My daughter's class at school was the first where Asians were in the majority. Now I'm talking about nice, well-behaved, hard-working kids. In lessons, no problems. But then, after school, the Asian kids went to each others' homes to do their homework together whilst my daughter and her friends went to the cinema and the shops. Nothing judgemental here; they simply didn't mix.

Integration is a fantasy, at least if you expect it to happen in any reasonable period of time. Why would anyone want to integrate anyway? Where's the mileage in it? People don't come to live in this country because they like our customs or admire our way of life. Not any more, if ever. They come for free schooling, free healthcare, and a welfare system to provide them with security in their old age. Plus, in some cases, the opportunity to get on in a way they could never hope to do at home. And why shouldn't they? Wouldn't you?

At least there now seems to be an acceptance at national and local levels that integration is not a realistic target. Not in our lifetime at any rate. So, as always, the pendulum swings too far the other way. Now, not only are differences in culture to be celebrated, they are to be cherished and encouraged. Hence, separate churches, multi-cultural recruiting, exceptions and allowances for dress and attire, multi-lingual teaching, separate classes, even separate schools – as well as a whole new raft of court cases where the sensitivities of cultural minorities might or might not have been offended. Accompanied, needless to say, by a new raft of lawyers to profit from it all. You see, again, here we are relying on the law to make it all work. It won't.

There may be legal solutions to legal problems, financial solutions to financial problems, but you have to find cultural solutions to cultural problems.

It is said that time is the great healer. If so, how long will it take? History is not encouraging. The Jews are still suffering for their treatment of Christ, the American Negro still carries the cross of slavery, the Red Indian still mourns the loss of his plains. Closer to home, the Scots still resent the English, in Ireland the Catholics are still at war with the Protestants, the once industrial North distrusts the landowners of the South and everyone wants self-government.

Really, what hope is there for the Hindus, Muslims, Buddhists and Africans? And we haven't even got round to language, one of the greatest cultural barriers of all. Suggest we get rid of minority languages and even the Welsh are up in arms!

We've got to stop it now.

Immigration is a separate issue. I don't know whether we really need a flow of people from overseas in order to keep the wheels of commerce turning but, if we do, we must accept that immigrants will settle for being lowly paid public servants for one generation if you're lucky – after that they want their kids to be accountants, lawyers, doctors and engineers. Who can blame them? But if we thought we could fill the jobs that we were too good for by opening up the gates to immigrants, we've got to realise it was a disastrously short-term policy. Assuming it was a policy and not just another way to raise more money for the exchequer.

If, on the other hand, (and it's a big if), there really is a case for saying that we need a constant flow of immigrants for economic reasons, let's recruit them from other European countries where customs, traditions, history and religion are more or less common to us all. There's enough of them who want to come here and they stand a damn sight better chance of fitting in.

In my opinion.

P.S. Another thought. It seems far-fetched but, just as the Scots and the Welsh are demanding their own 'territory' back, is it conceivable that, in the fullness of time, our ethnic minorities will ask for areas of the country to be specifically designated for them? It would only be an extension of 'respecting' their right to have their own schools, churches, community centres, etc. Somewhere for them to live and enjoy the benefits of living in this country without having to mix with people they fundamentally disagree with. The

Muslims could have Middlesex, the Afro-Carribeans might like to take over South London and the Chinese could have Soho. Of course, this process is already well under way, the only change would be that they get to govern themselves. I would say they have as much right to this with their very real cultural and religious requirements as the Welsh and the Scots, wouldn't you?

Headmaster Malim Abdul Habib was killed by members of the Taliban for teaching girls in school.

Political Correctness
(Here's a hot potato!)

SORRY, but isn't this just a posh way of telling us we can't say what we think? That we've lost the 'right' to free speech?

Perhaps we should start by asking whether we ever had free speech in the first place, or was it just an illusion? Remember what happened at school if you indulged in a little free speech? Tell the class bully he was a fat prat and you'd be lying on your back with a black eye before you could say 'discoloured'. I don't remember getting on much better with the teachers. On the several occasions I revealed what I thought about them or their teaching methods, I seem to recall being on the wrong end of a detention (or in earlier years, a cane) with precious little time to exercise my right to reply.

What did that teach me? It taught me manners. It taught me courtesy. It taught me that it probably wasn't a good idea to offend and upset people because, more often than not, they would 'offend' me back and it would hurt - nothing noble about that, simply cowardliness and the desire for a quiet life. But it didn't teach me respect.

You see, if we all respected and were courteous to one another we wouldn't need 'political correctness' - in fact, we wouldn't need lots of things, new laws for example. But we don't. The truth is that people have bad qualities as well as good ones. Anyway respect is a consequence not a project.

Say you bump into someone you know who is blonde and beautiful but also lazy and selfish. Prior experience may not have led you to respect her particularly, but good manners dictate that you comment on her charm and beauty, not call her a lazy cow. You don't need to be told that. So long as she hasn't done you any harm, to offend would be pointless. This simple application of common sense gets us through ninety per cent of personal encounters ninety per cent of the time. We used to call it politeness (which could almost be shorthand for 'political correctness', couldn't it?)

The trouble comes when, firstly, you've had a bad experience as a result of something the woman has said or done and, secondly, when you start to think all beautiful blondes are the same. Now, every time you meet a gorgeous blonde you will be far less inclined to be polite. You might even be tempted to utter that fateful phrase: "Oh, I've met your type before, you blondes are all the same!" Stupid, yes. Unusual, no.

And yet, and yet...

It would be nice to think that everyone is a complete individual, different in every way, unique in all regards. But, is it true? Come to think of it, I'd be pushed to say the beautiful blondes I've known haven't displayed certain traits and characteristics. Similarly redheads. I'm not saying there *aren't* redheads who don't have a temper but I don't know one.

The truth is that we *want* to group people together. It makes life simpler. In fact, we celebrate group characteristics. Northerners are proud to be different to southerners. The Scots are different to the Irish, the French to the Spanish and so on. But these are the good differences not the bad ones. It's one thing to say that Northerners are hard workers, industrious and community spirited, quite another to say they're dull, stupid and dirty. Tell the French that, as a race, they are suave, romantic and sophisticated and they'll purr with pleasure, tell them they are arrogant, manipulative and stink of garlic and they'll shove you back into La Manche quicker than you can say Maurice Chevalier.

This is where political correctness comes in. All it's really saying is that we should be nice to one another – whether we like each other or not. Don't generalise. We can say as many complimentary things about each other as we like – individually or collectively – but we mustn't be horrid, especially if we are attributing people's bad qualities to their race, colour or creed. Not a bad idea you might think, if not particularly original.

But, we shouldn't need laws to enforce it.

"Perhaps he thought I was going to throw bread rolls, drink too much lemonade and sing rap loudly with my hood up."
61 YEAR OLD WOMAN ASKED TO LEAVE A KENT
RESTAURANT BECAUSE HER M&S TOP HAD A HOOD

The Quango Effect

*Do you ever get the feeling we're not being governed
by the government anymore? I picked up a cab in
Wandsworth not long ago and had a conversation with
the driver which led me to a possible explanation.*

THE Quango Effect. Sounds like a sci-fi movie, doesn't
it? For one of the most disliked words in the language you'd
think 'quango' meant Christmas to this government.

What a perfect way to run things. Never mind the Civil
Service with its independence and freedom of thought,
cultivated and preserved by successive governments of all
political flavours for centuries. Trouble is they ask questions,
argue and simply won't do as they're told. Far better to
appoint new committees, new 'departments' and staff them
with people carefully chosen to reflect and promote the
current politically correct agenda of the small coterie of
politicians running the show, then give them the legal powers
to enforce it.

The fact that this agenda has never been presented as part
of any manifesto, or voted on by the electorate is ruthlessly
ignored. After all, what do we know?

Fact. We've got more quangos today than ever before,
spreading their tentacles into every branch of our lives from
education to healthcare, gambling to local government.

Dictating policy and costing huge sums of public money. Last year we had nearly a thousand non-elected government bodies employing nearly 100,000 staff. And it's no secret that Labour activists are three times more likely to be appointed to quangos than their Conservative counterparts.

If you are still wondering why political correctness is so dominant in modern Britain when everyone thinks it's ridiculous, then blame the sinister influence of the quangos. Make no mistake, this is Big Brother come true.

The danger is that we grumble and moan in typically British fashion without doing anything, on the assumption that sooner rather than later common sense will prevail and it will all go away. Don't count on it. This country is not what it was, nor is it run in the same way. The lunatics really are running the asylum and quangos are both their strike force and their cover.

Let's just remind ourselves what we are talking about here. In the most outrageous way our 'elected' government – with less than half the votes of the total electorate - is subverting democracy by appointing cronies to existing and newly-established publicly-funded bodies backed up by legal powers to implement half-baked political ideologies which, in most cases, have *not even been debated in Parliament.*

Quangos are simply a structured way of making sure that your mates run the show the way you want them to. Without saying for a moment that previous governments haven't used the same methods to avoid the inconvenience of having to argue and win their case, none have done so on the epic scale of this government or stuffed the system so unashamedly with chums, flatmates, relatives and family members.

I remember someone once saying how much easier it would be to run the railways if you didn't have to worry about the trains. Well, now we have a so-called democratically elected government who have found a way to do what they want without having to be democratic.

Talk about government by stealth.

Last year quangos cost the taxpayer £35 billion a year, a rise of £10 billion since New Labour came to power.

Education

FACT: 44% of our 11-year olds fail to reach the basic requirement in reading, writing and arithmetic. Here's a topic which gets everyone frowning, especially when there has been a news story about holding bright kids back to make the less bright ones feel better.

I met a University professor recently who told me that universities are recruiting lecturers on the basis of their research skills and not their teaching. In fact, he said most of them don't even want to teach. They regard it as interfering with their more important work of getting academic articles published and securing research grants. When asked why this was, he explained that all the universities get more money from research than they do from teaching and educating students. Plus, it's research that gives universities kudos in 'the marketplace'.

Now, I didn't know there was a 'marketplace' – somehow I'd always assumed that educating our kids was more important than that. But, apparently, I was wrong.

"So," I asked, "you're working in a university, what are you going to do about it?" "There's nothing I can do," was his reply, "it's the funding bodies, you see, they won't give money to universities who don't excel at research – and, without the funding, we'd go to the wall."

But, the funding is provided by the Government, isn't it? Shouldn't they be funding education first and foremost, not research? In fact, why should there be a fight between the two in the first place? Isn't it possible to have both properly funded, working hand in hand? "Doesn't seem to work like that," was the professor's reply.

It never does, does it?

I don't know about you, but do you think your kids are cleverer than you? Better educated? Smarter? I don't. Try to remember what you were like at their age, what you were good at, how much you knew, and then compare yourselves to them. You may feel you didn't have much of an education, but you've done well enough to give your kids a better schooling than you had yourself. Well done, and good luck to you. Even so, they may *know* more than you did, but are they cleverer? How's their work ethic? Do they put in the hours that you did, has their 'better' education prepared them better for life? In short, where has our education system got us in the last half century?

I asked a friend this the other day. He thought hard before saying: "Well, they can work computers and I couldn't at their age." When I reminded him there weren't any computers when he was their age, well, I ask you.

You see, despite what we're told by politicians, our education system is no better now than it was in the 50's. Arguably, it's worse. So, is this a continuing failure by successive governments - or could it be intentional? Seems impossible, doesn't it? But remember, a stupid population is a lot easier to govern than a clever one. Especially when the people doing the governing might not be too bright themselves.

Conspiracy theories aside, no-one can deny the fact that our education system is in a mess. The more the politicians meddle, the worse it gets. And throwing money at the problem doesn't help either. It never does. As soon as the State starts paying for something, then the political agenda of the day comes into play. It's the price we pay for 'free' education and 'free' healthcare. Not that it's really free since it comes out of our taxes but, because the cash is routed via the government, they get to run it and we don't. By 'we' I mean the punters who, in the case of education, are the parents.

I've heard it said by 'experts' that if the price you pay for equality of education is that the bright kids lose out, then so be it. How can that possibly make sense? Again, it's putting political ideology ahead of the practicalities of living in the modern world. Surely it's obvious we need as many bright people as we can get.

I once read that the UK had the lowest average intelligence of all the European countries but the highest percentage of extremely intelligent individuals. At first, that may sound like a contradiction, but think again. It makes sense. You see, it's that relatively small group of very bright people that has got this country where it is. The Germans, for example, are brighter than us across the board but, over the years, we've had a few more really clever people and that's made all the difference. That's why we've been able to outfox them more than once, politically, militarily and commercially. That is why this country led the world in so many areas, despite the fact that we are a tiny island with a relatively small population.

Now, of course, everything has changed. Why? Because other countries have copied our best ideas over and over again, and one of those ideas has been the way we used to educate our kids. Letting the bright ones get ahead, indeed, concentrating effort on getting the very best out of them, even more than they would otherwise achieve despite their intellectual head start. Stretch them, make it hard for them, academically, physically and spiritually. Challenge them to apply and exercise their minds. Push them to do even better. If they're bright enough they'll respond and reach, even exceed, their immediate potential. Needless to say that doesn't mean we should ignore the rest - that would be very stupid indeed. But, for God's sake, don't bring the bright ones down to some artificial politically underpinned common denominator. Therein lies mediocrity and decline.

Neither does the ideology help the less bright kids. It goes like this: we're all born equal so there is no such thing as bright kids or stupid kids. And, what's more, even if there are, we must not treat one group differently to the other. Mix them all together and the less advantaged will be better off by sitting alongside the bright ones. Somehow their 'brightness' will rub off. Hogwash. Here's why.

Example. I'm having a tea party. The guests include Paris Hilton, Kate Moss, Madonna, Naomi Campbell and Jerry Hall. Oh yes, and my neighbour Pam who happens to be fourteen stone, looks like Margaret Rutherford and is living off benefits. She's going to feel great, isn't she? No, she won't. The reality is the experience would be humiliating for her, she wouldn't feel comfortable and would probably end up disliking, almost certainly resenting, and quite possibly hating the others. Sorry, I know that this will offend the politically correct amongst you, but the chances are that the quicker my neighbour Pam can get the hell out of there and back to a group of people she can be comfortable with the happier she will be. It's common sense that youngsters will learn more and grow more confident in groups of similar ability.

The trouble is intelligence is genetic. You get bright parents with thick children and, happily, vice versa. No-one knows quite why, but that's the way it is. To pretend they're all the same is nonsense. Tragically, the consequences are that *neither the less intelligent nor brighter ones get the education they deserve.* We're letting them all down because of political ideology - and hypocrisy. You've read about cabinet ministers, supposedly committed to state education, sending their kids to private schools.

You may, of course, take a different view. You may believe that it's preferable to give kids an easier time, less stressful, less competitive. If we stopped driving our kids so hard, wouldn't they grow up more pleasant, less aggressive, nicer and more considerate to others? Possibly – as long as you confine your thinking to within these shores. The trouble is that at the very time we are relaxing our educational standards, so the emerging countries of the world are tightening up theirs. Even in the new 'global' society, in which we must all play some part, it would be a waste if we didn't bring to the table the fruits of our past successes, coupled with the talents, knowledge and experience gained over centuries of being in the forefront of science, technology and culture. To do this we need a hard-working education system.

What's more, it could be said that it is precisely because of our island history, out relative 'smallness' in the grand scheme of things, that we need to be brighter, cleverer than everyone else. After all, we can only submit ourselves to free competition within a global market if have a reasonable expectation of occasionally coming out on top. Politics, politics. It really shouldn't interfere with the overriding objective of providing every child, regardless of ability, with the best possible chance of reaching his or her full potential. But, it does.

Tell me anyone in their right mind who would put political agendas ahead of education? Talk about the politics of envy! "I can't get a good education for my kids, so you can't have one either." Tosh. Leave schools alone. Let them get on with it and we'll soon see who can attract and keep the best teachers, who can produce the best results. Okay, so it's not perfect and you will get winners and losers – we get them anyway. What matters is that, over time, things get better, not worse. This hasn't been happening.

It may not be fair, but then what is? At the end of the day, constant intervention by successive governments, both left and right, has not improved education in this country. They've tried everything. Shutting down Grammar schools, starting them up again, changing exam systems, changing them back, discouraging private schools, setting endless targets, messing around with the syllabus, taking away and re-introducing the three R's, abolishing streaming, bringing it back. Even using social engineering to manipulate university entrance. Did you know there is a quango called the Fair Access Regulator who tells universities how to introduce social engineering into their admissions policies? Isn't it outrageous to make it difficult for kids from private schools to get university places? How dare they discriminate against *any* group of kids – it's simply not their fault. None of it has worked and none of it will. Government will never solve the problem of education because government itself *is* the problem.

Education should have nothing to do with politics. It should be above politics. Good education is about acquiring knowledge, facts, broadening experience, appreciation, understanding and opportunity – helping children become adults so that they can develop ideas of their own, not cramming them with dodgy dogma. The objective of good education is not to produce a co-operative, acquiescent electorate, but to equip youngsters for worthwhile, productive, independent lives. Do that and they will become good citizens, too. It certainly isn't about turning children into good little socialists, conservatives or anything else. This is silly, dangerous.

For the educational process to succeed, more than anything, it is about the relationship a child has with a teacher. It's a very special thing, a bit like parent and child. No-one really knows why some of these relationships work and others don't. It's like magic. And when you come across it, stand back in wonder, admire and then - *leave it alone!*

Leave the teaching to teachers. Let them be individuals, let them inspire, impart their knowledge and compassion and, with luck, their wisdom and experience. We know some of them won't toe the party line, you're going to get a few communists and anarchists – even the odd old-fashioned right or left winger - but it's a small price to pay for being on the receiving end of someone who sees teaching as a vocation.

I've seen kids with little or no academic ability and not a lot of natural intelligence, tearaways really, enthralled and engrossed by one teacher and then, minutes later, seriously taking the piss out of another. The kids are the same, it's the teacher that's different. I don't know how to produce more good teachers but it's something to do with recruiting people who (a) really want to do it (b) have the character and maturity to command the kids' respect and (c) are well rewarded for the job. Kids won't learn if they don't want to and they won't learn from someone who they sense has nothing of real value to teach them.

If you haven't got good teachers, no amount of interfering, busy-bodying, messing with budgets, syllabuses, exams, structures, buildings and systems will make any difference. To produce well-educated kids you've got to have well-educated teachers. Without either you're on a downward spiral. I hope someone sees this before it's too late.

In the meantime it's every man for himself. Make the best decisions you can for your child and don't let yourself be lulled into thinking there's a well-oiled machine out there ready and able to take the responsibility for your child growing up away from you. There isn't. There may be a good school near you. If there is you're lucky – move heaven and earth to get your kid in. If there isn't, think about moving yourself. Think what's important.

My old man used to say to me that I hadn't asked to be born. He was right. Having kids is entirely the parents' idea. The least you can do is put yourself out for them.

And let's bring back streaming. Urgent.

P.S. Does anyone else have niggling doubts about women teaching boys and men teaching girls? I know that we've had mixed sex schools for a long time but it does seem to me implausible to expect strapping seventeen year old boys not to want sex with beautiful twenty-one year old female teachers and vice versa. Similarly, we have more reported cases of older teachers of both sexes seducing pupils under the age of consent. Mixed sex schools with mixed sex teachers were brought in at a time when we did not have the relaxed and liberal attitude to sex we have now. When I was at school men taught boys and women taught girls – a lot less distracting all round with far less temptation served up on a plate.

If I was a fourteen year-old boy at the receiving end of sex lessons (as prescribed by our far-sighted and visionary leaders) from a gorgeous twenty-one year old woman it would seem like gratuitous soft porn courtesy of the state.

What a turn-up! What a turn-on.

"76% of British people believe that the brightest pupils should be taught separately and pushed harder. They don't resent this as elitism: it just makes good, practical sense."
SURVEY BY THE CENTRE FOR POLICY STUDIES, JANUARY 2007

Universities

Opinions vary about university education - although it seems that all parents whose kids go to university are proud enough when they get in. The problems seem to start when they leave.

ALTHOUGH I never went to a university, I always thought they were a good idea - for some.

Now, of course, everyone goes to university and things have changed out of all recognition as a result.

All three of my kids went to university. All three agree it was harder to get 'A' Levels at school than degrees. Not that this is necessarily a bad thing providing they get something of real value out of the experience, but taking three or four years out of a young life to loaf around picking up bad habits (like borrowing and living in debt) certainly is.

When I was twenty-two, the time when these bright young things start work if they're lucky, I'd already been working for five years! I was a seasoned pro by the time they were going for their first job interviews.

I can't speak for anyone else, but when my three left university, they had no better idea what they wanted to do next than when they left school. In fact, two of them – along with a number of their friends – said they thought the whole thing was a waste of time despite leaving with second-class honours. While they could have been out there experiencing the University of Life, they were going through the motions of being grown up and exercising their independence while, in reality, they were simply guinea pigs in the Great Social Experiment and keeping the jobless total down.

There was a time when universities set out to be centres of excellence. Places where bright, intelligent young people would go to get even smarter. I've got no problem with that. The more knowledgeable the few, the better it is for the many.

We really do have to get used to this idea all over again. You're always going to have a small number of people running the shop, so the smarter they are the better. There's only one thing worse than being bossed around by people who are cleverer than you are and that's being bossed around by people who are stupid.

The idea of universities and public schools was to produce exactly those 'clever' people. It explains the way they work. I was talking to a kid the other day who had just started at university. He was surprised they didn't have to go to lectures unless they wanted to. That's a leftover from the past when the idea was that those who were fortunate enough to be there had a thirst for knowledge, a desire to learn. Now, of course, half of them don't bother.

Don't get me wrong: I'm all for kids from all social backgrounds having the opportunity to go to university. It's not their backgrounds that matter, it's their attitude – and aptitude. Let's face it, if they're not interested in learning by the time they are eighteen, they're not suddenly going to turn into Stephen Hawking just because they're been sent to what used to be called Croydon Tech. OK, maybe that's a bit extreme, but the people who run the universities aren't magicians and they can't do transformations.

No, what has happened, and will continue to happen, is that universities have had to change to suit their new-style customers. It's a fact of life that standards invariably drop to the lowest common denominator; they seldom if ever rise to the highest. Now we've got so many universities – every technical college and polytechnic I knew as a youngster is now called a university – and so many courses, many of which would have once been classified as hobbies and pastimes - there's a real danger that a university education is not merely a waste of time but positively harmful. After all, what could be worse than leaving university less well equipped to deal with the harsh reality of working for a living than before!

Needless to say, like all other institutions, universities are under incredible pressure from the politicians. In fact, we are rapidly getting to the point where the whole of our education system is not about acquiring knowledge but about instilling political and ideological beliefs. For the first time in living memory we are governed by people so certain they know what is best for us that they want to control the way we think from cradle to grave. In terms of education that means from kindergarten through to the time we leave the education system.

The government also wants to keep unemployment figures down. Keeping as many seventeen to twenty one years olds as possible at university and out of the job market makes a sizeable contribution.

The hypocrisy is mind-boggling. For example, we've had a Minister of Education who is a proclaimed Catholic, in fact, a member of Opus Dei. This means by definition that she is fundamentally opposed to contraception and the practises of homosexuals. Yet, under her supervision, both contraception and the tolerance of gays within the community are being actively promoted in our schools, the same minister incidentally who, having consistently campaigned against private education, chose to send her own child to private school. I must say I have a higher regard for her private decisions than I do for her public and professional ones. When presented with a conflict of this nature the solution is simple - resign. But then politicians don't do that anymore, do they?

Where were we? Oh yes. Fortunately, one way or another, the few really bright youngsters we have, those with a real appetite for learning and self-improvement, will find their way through all this nonsense and will have something to say about the way things will be done in the future. They may even be clever enough to stop meddling in things they don't understand and leave the rest of us to get on with running our own lives.

That is unless we drive them all overseas. We've had 'brain drains' in the past which have cost this country dear, and we may have them again.

"Going to university can speed mental decline. Graduates may get 'overwhelmed' with information and suffer greater memory loss in later life."
EILEEN CRIMMINS, UNIVERSITY OF SOUTHERN CALIFORNIA

The United States of Europe

*I've never met a taxi driver who believes that the European
Project is a good idea. Put this down to patriotism
if you like, but there's plenty of argument from the
back of a taxi, much of it pro-Europe, and it's failed to
convince the majority of drivers I've come across.*

DID you know there are twenty-five countries and 450 million
people in the EU? Why should you? In fact, you probably
know very little about the EU. Nor do I. That's because
nobody took the trouble to explain it to us in the first place.

The creation and growth of the European Superstate will
go down in history as the biggest example of political stealth
since Churchill, Roosevelt and Stalin carved up Europe
after the 2nd Word War. It has had nothing to do with
the wishes of ordinary people and everything to do with
the grand visions of politicians who saw an unprecedented
opportunity for undreamt of power and glory. Consultation,
argument and persuasion were never on the menu. This
was all far too important and complicated for the common
man to grasp. So, instead of what is now referred to as the
"European Debate" (which was never allowed to happen),
they just got on with it, certain in the knowledge that it was
best for us all. Whether we wanted it or not. The Danes
voted against the Maastricht Treaty in 1992. The result

was ignored and they were made to vote again the following year. Demonstrators against the second poll were shot in the streets. Only recently Tony Blair and Gordon Brown withdrew plans for a referendum on the euro in the UK because they knew they would lose.

Do you remember how it all started? We were going to have a free-trade zone. No duty on fags and alcohol, no passports, no import controls. It was called the Common Market. Well, I ask you, who wouldn't vote for that?

The fact is most of us are still blissfully unaware that Ted Heath was committed to a single currency by 1976 (...ah, so that was what decimalisation was all about...) or that our gold reserves have long since been shipped off to Germany. Missed that, did you? Well, it was in Maastricht and that nice Mr Major signed up to it. Like everything else to do with the Community this ultimate and irreversible act of surrender was conducted covertly and if you've got any questions save them til afterwards, lad.

Anyway, we're still thinking about it, aren't we? Maybe we want in, maybe we don't. We'll make up our minds later. In the meantime, whatever happened to the Common Market? Good idea, that. Away with duties, customs, red tape and unnecessary bureaucracy making it difficult to sell our goods freely to our European neighbours. The trouble is it's all still there, much of it worse than ever. Instead of losing petty restrictions, we've lost the war of independence. The CM became the EEC, the EEC turned into the European Federation and the EF was re-named the EU. Soon we'll have the United States of Europe – which was the original idea anyway. And, it's only taken thirty years! Brilliant, if you like that sort of thing.

We've thrown in our lot - firstly to comfort a generation prepared to sacrifice anything rather than risk another war in Europe and then to feed the ambitions of politicians who foresaw a glorious future for themselves as part of the hierarchy of a much greater world power. The trouble is nobody told us. What should have been a collection of nation states united by a common purpose, has ended up a continent divided, worse, in truth, a continent misled.

Even the Channel Tunnel, the umbilical cord and symbol of Britain's new attachment to 'the continent', turned out to be a half-hearted affair. When we should have been driving ourselves under the short stretch of sea between Folkestone and Calais unencumbered save, perhaps, for a fairly hefty toll, here we are loading four-wheeled vehicles perfectly capable of self-propulsion onto other larger and clumsier wheeled vehicles thus necessitating precisely the same loading, ticketing and safety procedures that you get with the ferries. Yes, Le Shuttle is a bit quicker, and perhaps we should be glad of that, but it's not actually what we wanted, is it?

I digress.

Here's something I don't understand, maybe you do. Why is a socialist Europe with a common agricultural policy, standardised employment law and working conditions, common taxation and a common currency good for trade? I don't see it. If a bread toaster made in Berlin costs the same to manufacture as a toaster made in Solihull, where's the trade? If workers everywhere are being paid the same and enjoying identical working conditions, where's the incentive to travel and re-locate? In the end all you're doing is eliminating competition between the countries of Europe. I can see that in the short term we might sell things to Turkey that they don't make themselves, but that's not going to last very long, is it? In the end – and I'm only talking twenty thirty years ahead – we'll get a kind of stalemate where everything will be the same everywhere and they'll be no gain for anyone.

Then what will happen? All the European countries will look outside the EU for cheap manufacturing, cheap labour and cheap prices. In other words, Europe will continue to exploit the poor and those prepared to suffer intolerable working conditions just as we always have, except now they'll be somewhere else. What a great moral victory for the socialists that will be.

Did I say: "Then what *will* happen'? Good grief, its happening already and on a vast scale, too. Every time you get a sales call from a double-glazing company or a telephone company you can be pretty certain that the person you are talking to is earning a fraction of his counterpart over here and probably living in a tin-roofed, one-bedroom shack in Bombay with his wife and six brothers and sisters. But that's okay because they're not in Europe. Talk about human rights.

This doesn't sound like the great economic and social miracle it was cracked up to be, does it? Remember all that talk about how we couldn't afford to live outside the EU because it would be 'disastrous for our economy'? Why should it be? We have the whole of the world to trade with and we're much better at it than our European neighbours, too. Which, in my opinion, is the main reason the others are so keen to keep us in – not because it will be better for us, but because it will clip our wings, rein us in and make them feel slightly better about their own performance in world markets. Plus, they want our money.

The politics of envy yet again.

Just as most Europeans were proved right when they opposed the Blair-Bush post-imperial war in Iraq, so they are against the post-imperial EU project.

JOHN LAUGHLAND, FORMER LECTURER IN POLITICS
AND PHILOSOPHY AT THE SORBONNE AND AT THE
INSTITUTE OF POLITICAL SCIENCE IN PARIS

Men and Women

*You can rely on some lively and generally light-hearted
banter on this topic, especially if yet another story
about women being better than men at practically
everything has been trailed across the front pages.*

LISTENING to politicians and reading the papers you'd
think that there is either no difference between the sexes
anymore or we've all become women. Men are no longer
'relevant' is a favourite view, leading on from the idea that
by some strange quirk of evolution during the last twenty
years or so, women have mutated into a super version of the
species who can do anything and everything we used to need
two sexes for. Men conspire in the illusion. Just look at TV
commercials that show women constantly on top, grinding
their stilettos into some unfortunate guy's neck, or belittling
men in an endless array of humiliating situations. By and
large men make these ads, so what's going on?

Back to basics. Men and women have been equipped
differently by nature for very good reasons. Both sexes have
good and not-so-good qualities, which are there for a purpose.
The problem is that not all these qualities are needed all of
the time.

We can trace these characteristics back to earlier times
before we'd surrounded ourselves with a man-made (no pun

intended) protectivist society designed to prevent most of us having to deal with extreme situations most of the time. In fact, man has been striving to protect his woman for thousands of years. It's a male thing. To succeed he's had to do some pretty awful stuff – like killing, beating and cheating. When your life is threatened, or more likely, the lives of your family, you don't stop to argue.

It also explains the male sense of humour. Men will have a laugh about anything. Men don't take things too seriously and aren't big on self-recrimination. When you've got to feed a starving family in a cave you don't worry about whether you've slaughtered an animal humanely under controlled conditions or, for that matter, if the carcass has been shared out fairly with your neighbours in the cave next door. Selfishness and survival are one and the same and when you've done something pretty disgusting it's useful to be able see the funny side of it - especially if there are a few mates around to share the joke. But don't expect the girls to join in. Most women can't even begin to understand the male sense of humour. They find it foul. Of course, they're quite right.

Human beings are equipped to function well in emergencies and in extreme conditions. It's one of the reasons our species has been so successful. Except that, in the process, we've become the victims of our own success. In more recent times we've not only become better at dealing with the extremes, we've managed to eliminate them all together. Now, we're left with all those primeval survival instincts with nothing to do with them most of the time. So, it's not men who have become irrelevant, it's the things they are good at.

But let's not get complacent.

The fact is that after thousands, millions of years, men have finally created a world (or at least a largish chunk of it), which is safe enough for female values to prevail. But this won't last forever. Nature has a remarkable knack of turning the tables. And we'd better make sure that our menfolk don't get so softened up that they won't be able to deal with horrid 'old-fashioned' males from elsewhere who could decide to be beastly to us at any time. The softer we allow ourselves to become, the more in touch with our 'feminine side', the easier target we become for bullies and fanatics.

That's why it's so important to keep sport going in schools. It's a way of keeping testosterone on a back burner – safely out of the way, but still in training should it be required in the real world. If governments don't see this, well, they should. And, for heaven's sake, let's keep females out of the armed services. Before you can say Boadicia you'll have armies led by people who think that wars can be won over a cup of tea and a chat. The trouble is those people will only be on one side. Be afraid.

Men are no more or less important than women. It simply happens that in the west, for the time being, male qualities are not so much in demand as they used to be. Ironically, that is not so much a consequence of women's lib (as the few remaining strident feminists would have us believe), but a result of a lot of hard work, by men, over a very long period of time. Men have worked their way out of a job – for now. It would be nice to think they won't be required to use their 'protective' qualities ever again but it doesn't sound likely, does it?

We assume that it's a modern idea for women to go out to work. I doubt that very much. Go back to the caves or the jungle and you'll find that all the young, fit members of the tribe would be expected to work. Male or female. It was the elders' job to look after the kids. That's where we've failed, you see. Grandparents aren't so keen to take the responsibility for the children anymore. In the year 2007 they are too busy enjoying their own 'quality time' – cruising, playing golf, popping off to the flat in Javea, going to the theatre – you name it. They're even less prepared to give up their hard-earned leisure time than the mums and dads! No-one in the family has got time to look after babies. So what happens? A new wave of au pairs, nannies, live-in helpers expands to fill the vacuum - if you can afford them. If not, you're stuck with local authority funded childcare and playgroups. Not ideal.

No, there's a lot to be said for preserving 'le difference'. If both sexes concentrate on what comes naturally to them, then the combination is both powerful and enjoyable. It's ridiculous that a woman thinks a man is stupid because he likes to use up his spare testosterone watching Chelsea beat ManU on a Saturday afternoon. Far better he does that than go out and get into a fight. Similarly, men should delight in the fact that women spend hours getting dressed, trying to look their best. If they're doing it for their partners and being appreciated, then they're not dong it for anyone else.

Men and women have to learn to enjoy being different from each other, not allow themselves to get wound up and angry, nor be fooled into thinking the grass is greener on the other side.

Nature intended the sexes to work together in harmony not be envious of each other. Nothing's changed.

"There is no unisex brain. Girls arrive already wired as girls and boys as boys. Their brains are what drives their impulses, values and their very reality."

DR LUAN BRIZENDINE, PSYCHIATRIST, UNIVERSITY OF LOS ANGELES

Common Sense

*Here's a quality well understood and prized by licensees of the
Public Carriage Office who wouldn't survive long without it. But
there's a distinct feeling that it's in increasingly short supply.*

NOT so long ago there was a directive to the judges from
Lord Wolf or Charlie Falconer or someone, whoever it is
that has the job of telling judges how to do their job. It went
roughly like this:

> "Judges are advised to avoid the phrase 'common sense'
> in addressing plaintiffs or to rely on common sense
> when arriving at judgements. This is because 'common
> sense' will have different meanings and connotations
> depending on culture, race, colour and creed"

That may not be the precise wording but that was the drift of
it. Judges shouldn't apply common sense anymore? Tell me
if I'm wrong, but that's what I thought judges did ninety per
cent of the time. A good judge using his brain and experience
will surely sift through all the contradictory arguments, red
herrings and false trails being presented to him by fiendishly
clever opposing barristers and come to a simple conclusion.
Guilty, not guilty or case not proved. Whatever. His job is
to see the wood for the trees. Tell him he can't apply his

common sense to the job and you're tying his hands behind his back. I would like to think most judges have sufficient common sense to ignore such a silly, 'pc'-motivated dictat.

What gets to people more than anything is when events appear to go against the tide of common sense. In fact, when things are so obviously not 'sensible', whether on the national or international stage or simply in your own backyard, all the cleverly assembled arguments in the world won't change your mind. What's more, common sense enjoys a broader parish than the Law Lords might think. Take the war in Iraq, for example. I don't know many people, regardless of culture, who think it is a good idea. Similarly, you'll find as much resistance against indiscriminate and illegal immigration amongst existing immigrants as from the rest of us. Come to think of it, I don't know anyone of any ethnic or cultural background who doesn't think you should be able to have a go at someone who breaks into your house.

At a more personal level, it can't be common sense for a parent to get to a stage where he's not on speaking terms with his own son. I've got a friend in this position. He's not stupid by any means – nor is his son - but he makes a really strong case why the two of them are better off not talking to each other. The son agrees. Listening to them you could almost be convinced they are right. But they're not. Because common sense tells you they should be trying really hard to get back together and that means talking to each other.

There are countless examples I can think of where common sense seems to be at odds with outcome. But one thing is certain, common sense at the most fundamental level is, quite literally, common – it's more widespread than you might think, in fact, most of us have it to some degree or another.

So, if common sense is so widely available, why do we so seldom see it applied to the things that matter? Obviously, something is getting in the way. Maybe lots of things. When someone says you'll make a fortune investing in some crazy business venture, common sense may tell you it's nonsense but greed may cause you to part with your money. Power is another thing. I was told by a taxi driver 'in the know' that when the decision was made by the cabinet to go ahead with the construction of the Millennium Dome, Tony Blair wasn't even there. Most cabinet members were against it and had put forward common sense arguments to support this view, until John Prescott said the Prime Minister was very much in favour and he thought the cabinet should support him. With that, the decision was taken to go ahead and, again, common sense went out the window.

Listening to others is another distraction. Especially so-called 'experts'. Here we run into another frequent enemy of common sense. It's called 'agenda'. I once tried to get my accountant to shut down some small companies I wasn't using anymore. I couldn't believe how much he argued the toss until I realised he was earning a fee every time he submitted a set of dormant accounts!

Lawyers are another obvious case in point. Why try to settle a case speedily and without undue distress to all concerned when you can double, treble your fees by dragging it out. Ask anyone who has been through a divorce. Common sense tells you that two people who once loved each other and were, possibly for years, good friends should be able to sort out their own separation and terms. Nevertheless, convention requires that one or other party goes to a solicitor to 'initiate' proceedings. Well, there's common sense out of the window, for sure!

To truly apply God's gift of common sense, you have to become largely impervious to the views of others. Not to the extent of not listening, but in terms of making decisions.

Others will try to change your mind, not always for unselfish reasons. What mother, for example, would encourage her children and grandchildren to emigrate? Not many, I'm sure. Understandable, but if common sense has led them to believe that the move would be in their best interests, then they must go whatever she thinks. Tough, but there it is.

Ask successful people how they rank the qualities that helped them get on. I bet you common sense – plus the ability to apply it - will be high on their list. It's the mad inventor syndrome. You can come up with a brilliant idea, but without the common sense to know what to do with it, the idea is worthless. I can remember at school how the 'clever' lads stood out – they should all have become leaders of society, politicians, rich businessmen, great actors, star sportsmen, etc. What happened? They were never heard of again. It was the others, the quiet ones, even the bad lads, not greatly gifted on the face of it, who went on to excel in later years. Why? Ask them and they'll tell you. They had common sense.

I'm well aware that, so far, I haven't attempted to say what common sense is. That's a hard one. But, if pressed, I would say that it is a combination of two things: understanding human nature and having the courage of your own convictions.

Let's take human nature first. All human beings are motivated by the same set of characteristics going right back to the beginning of things. So, at level one, you have (a) the need to survive (b) the need to reproduce and (c) the need to do our best for ourselves and our kids.

Sounds simple – surely life is more complicated than that? Yes, but it is surprising how much of our day-to-day behaviour stems from these fundamental necessities. Of course, as our species has developed, so our motivations have become less obvious and more sophisticated, but much of our lives is still dictated by the needs to survive, reproduce and nurture our offspring. Now, you might say this is no more than a recipe for selfishness. True. But everything we do to help others (unselfish) is helping the community around us to remain intact and provide us with the protection we need (selfish). In fact, it is the instinct to nourish and cherish those around us that has made us what we are. We are a gregarious lot, relatively weak and insignificant as individuals, yet, collectively, strong to the point of being invulnerable.

But living in groups has its drawbacks. Apart from anything else, we are not all the same. And, by heck, don't we make a lot of our differences? And that's where having the courage of our convictions comes into it. As Kipling said, if you can keep your head when all about you are losing theirs, well, you'll be a man my son. Being able to involve yourself in the group, with all its contradictory ideas and opinions, and yet to be able to stand back and rely on your own instincts and beliefs, is possibly the key to navigating your own way through the stormy ocean of life. Sounds easy, but it isn't. Shorthand for that knack is common sense.

I once knew a man who sat at Churchill's right hand at Chartwell in 1938 when the great man and his top-level aids were trying to work out what to do about Yugoslavia. The unanimous view around the table was that the allies should support the incumbent leader. My man, a brigadier still in his late twenties, thought that the decision was being arrived at too quickly, too glibly and too obviously. He chirped in with a different idea. How about getting behind a young rebel leader who, at the time, was hiding out in the hills. The others wanted to know what possible value there could be in that suggestion. He went on to explain that, with help and encouragement, the rebel might be persuaded to side with the allies against Germany whereas it was likely that the incumbent would adopt at best a neutral attitude, at worst support Hitler. Gradually, one by one, the others came round to this point-of-view. The decision was reversed and, within days, the young brigadier had been parachuted into the mountains of central Europe to locate the rebel leader and talk to him. That rebel was Tito and the young brigadier was Fitzroy Maclean who went on to ride beside Tito when he finally and victoriously marched into Belgrade.

Fitzroy referred to this ability to think for yourself, even when those around you were going in the opposite direction, as the 'spirit of contradiction'. He wrote about it often. He said it was essential to have at least one person sitting at the table who had the guts to go against the majority view, would not be intimidated and who would argue the opposing case. That's what I mean by having the courage of your convictions. Without it, you'll seldom be able to apply common sense.

Time is another enemy of common sense. The late Enoch Powell said that when the chips were down he had learned to rely on his brain. It was just that sometimes it took longer to come up with the answer. That makes sense. Feed a computer a simple problem, it will solve it in a split second. Give it something more complicated and it will grind away for several minutes. In this respect the brain is no different. Unfortunately, we've got used to the idea that there should be an instant solution to every problem. We live in a world of sound bites and quick fixes. Consequently, we don't give our brains the time they need to solve difficult or important problems.

The first thing is to know what is important and what isn't. Most things aren't - make a quick decision by all means, if you're wrong it won't make much difference anyway. But from time to time you'll come up against a situation where, depending upon your decision, the outcome may affect the rest of your life and probably others', too. And, if you're wrong, 'sorry' won't be good enough.

Assuming you are able to spot the difference (and we all know people who can't) then give the serious question more time. The more momentous it is, the more time your brain will need to dwell on it. "Sleep on it," is a good idea. Don't let others rush you. Tell them they'll have to wait, however irritating they may find it.

Of course, this can all be used to another end. Clever chairmen of boards and committees know how to plan agendas so that the important issues are sandwiched between or follow the simple ones. Burying a difficult item at the end of a long agenda is one way to guarantee that a proposal will go through 'on the nod'. Unsuspecting members will not be inclined to give it the time it deserves or to see it's significance. They may be bored by then or just plain tired. Their main thought is to get home.

Common sense needs room to breathe. Remember, you're not a genius. Few people are and the one I knew had no common sense whatsoever! There's no hurry, even though it may suit others to make you think there is.

Finally, once you've made your decision, don't expect everyone else to agree with it. Or that you'll be popular. Or even liked. None of this means you are wrong. You might be, you might not. Usually only time will tell.

Here's an example.

Common sense dictates that we have to make the best of human nature and not expect to be able to change it. Look at history and you'll see that those who attempted to do so, from Jesus to Hitler, all came to a sticky end. Realise that if people are being greedy, selfish, conniving, whatever, they're only displaying the very qualities that Nature equipped them with to survive in the first place. The trick is to harness all this for the greater good. That's what makes a great leader - and you know the best bit? The rest of us won't even know we are being led. What you can't do is create obstacles, pin people down, hem them in, invent more and more rules and regulations, destroy the very force that drives them in the first place – all in a futile attempt to get them to toe the line. In other words, to stop them being human beings. That's common sense, isn't it?

I've gone on a bit about it because it's important. Common sense needs to prevail if we are going to get ourselves out of some of the quandaries we're in.

Let's hope it's still out there in sufficient quantities.

The Met accused two tube workers of biting the heads of black jelly babies in a 'racially intimidating manner'. After two and a half years and £250,000 it took a jury 58 minutes to decide that the charges were fantastically stupid.

Lawyers

Well, they use taxis a lot - so that's something to be said for them!

THE rapid growth of the legal profession is an indication that we are trying to run society by attempting to make and enforce more and more rules and regulations.

It's also a sign of frustration. When democracy breaks down, when the consensus upon which it is based has gone, there is no longer enough time for the process of persuasion. While we are arguing the toss about immigration and cultural divides (yes, it would be great to convince terrorists that when they kill people they won't necessarily go to heaven) people are getting murdered in their thousands. This is when politicians run out of patience. In the end the Government is only left with three weapons – money, the law and the army. As we have learned the hard way, throwing money at problems seldom helps so, assuming that things aren't so out of hand that we are at the point of civil war, that leaves the law.

Naturally, modern day governments are finding themselves up against it when it comes to actually governing – a situation they have brought entirely upon themselves. A whole list of mismanaged and fudged decision-making, principally in the last thirty years, has left us dangerously close to an ungovernable society. That's not to say it isn't worse elsewhere but, compared to the luxury of the working democracy we have enjoyed for the last hundred years – and which was, incidentally, the envy of the civilised world - what we have now is a travesty.

All the major issues of the last quarter century have contributed to the breakdown of the consensus. The mistaken belief that we require an endless flow of immigrants to somehow keep our population levels up and drive the bottom end of the economy, the outdated 'free' thinking of the sixties and seventies which has played havoc with our education system, not to mention moral standards, the decline of the Church and the derision with which it is regarded by the state, the lampooning of the Royal Family and the Establishment, the emergence of government by media – not to mention the 'lowest common denominator' effect of throwing in our lot with a load of (by our old standards) corrupt ex-enemies – all of this has produced a breakdown of society into a huge number of stubborn and mostly ill-informed conflicting minorities, all of whom put their own self-interest ahead of the greater interests of the majority.

Not surprising, then, that lawyers have a hey-day and that government relies more and more on the law to arbitrate and decide who is right and who is wrong. After all, without the Church to provide guidance, who else do we turn to? I was brought up to believe that you only use the law as a last resort, the presumption being that sensible people should be able to agree a compromise without it - the so-called and much admired 'British compromise'. Of course, not only does government have the option of leaning on lawyers to enforce existing laws and statutes more rigorously, it also has the power to influence sentences and, in extreme cases, to change existing laws and invent new ones. Except the cases don't have to be extreme any more.

Take two examples: firstly, the persecution of the motorist. You might have thought that with the rapidly-expanding popularity of motor-cars since the last war – coupled with increasing prosperity - successive governments would have realised that the days of public transport were numbered and that the obvious task ahead was to embark upon a major programme of road building coupled with the re-development of city centres to accommodate individual and independent transport. Not a bit of it. In fact, quite the reverse. In contrast to the rest of Europe and America billions were ploughed into public transport, few roads were built, city centres became grid-locked and the motorist became public enemy number one. Cue lights and music for one of the most unnecessary and discriminatory political and legal campaigns of all time. Taxes on petrol went through the roof, huge policing resources were deployed against hapless motorists, parking was made near impossible or prohibitively expensive (causing huge damage to local shops and amenities), speed cameras were randomly sited throughout the country, not to mention the introduction of congestion charging and all manner of additional fines and offences. Add to this the red herring of damage to the environment and the ozone layer, none of it scientifically proven, and you have a war on your hands. If the government could make the motorist feel any more like a convicted criminal I would like to know how. But I'm sure they'll think of something. No coincidence either that all these measures just happened to produce huge additional revenues for local and national government.

Why? Because politicians decided that the car was bad for us and, since they couldn't stop us owning and driving them, they'd make it as difficult as possible for us to do so. Of course, for government that's the easy bit and, if we could accept that the principle was right in the first place (which

I don't), you could argue that it has been hugely successful. Except, has it? Latest figures show that we have more cars on the road than ever before and yet still the lowest investment in roads and car-related facilities in the developed world. Meanwhile, the other part of the equation, namely improving public transport, has, surprise, surprise, proved completely beyond the capability of any government in the last forty years.

Take another example. We are currently seeing one of the most sinister manipulations of power witnessed this century as our government seeks the removal of legislation designed to protect the privacy and freedom of the individual in the name of it's so-called 'fight' against terrorism. A 'fight' we would not have had in the first place had our esteemed Prime Minister not led us into the madness of an illegal war. As it is, we are now supposed to believe (a) that in order to prevent further acts of terrorism, the police need new powers to arrest (kill?) and put suspected terrorists behind bars without trial and (b) that we should all carry identity cards so that big brother knows exactly what we are doing at all times. "If you've got nothing to hide," they argue, "then you've got nothing to worry about." How come, then, we've never needed these measures before, not during the darkest periods of the last two wars, not during the atrocities of Northern Ireland, not, in fact, since Magna Carta?

Don't forget that income tax was introduced as a temporary measure. It's not even suggested that these measures will be temporary, to be withdrawn when the terrorist threat recedes! Don't be fooled, the government wants to be able to dispense summary justice as it sees fit and, given these powers, will find a whole host of opportunities to do so. If you think this is alarmist, remember the 82-year old heckler who was forcibly ejected from the Labour Party conference last year *under the new anti-terrorist laws?* If that doesn't send a chill down your spine, nothing will.

Identity cards are a way of keeping us all under surveillance, to make sure we pay our taxes and can't escape the beady eye of bureaucracy. We know through experience that measures of this sort rarely achieve their purpose, quite the reverse in fact, they often result in the exact opposite! Imagine the feast of opportunities that identity cards present to thieves and fraudsters - your entire life history contained in a chip on a piece of plastic, available to clone and copy at will. But, no doubt, we'll still end up with them.

None of this would be possible without the co-operation of the legislature and you can be sure that, after a flurry of symbolic protest, the lawyers will fall into line. Ever on hand, ever attentive and ever ready to gulp up monstrous amounts of public and private money turning spurious political ideology into law and, ultimately, convictions and punishments. It's like being back at school, isn't it? Something lawyers love beyond all else is new laws. Suddenly, it's Christmas!

Now, let's get up close and personal. It is often said that lawyers are the least popular of the professionals and no wonder. Lawyers thrive on the failures and misfortunes of others and, on the basis that for every winner there's a loser, at least half of their clients end up disappointed. That's not a great track record, is it?

Lawyers deal in the here and now. Life goes on and on for the rest of us and then, for some reason, we find ourselves dealing with a lawyer. We all know that context is everything. The same disagreement takes on a completely different significance depending upon the nature and intent of the parties involved. Yet it goes without saying the lawyer knows nothing of the pond in which this ripple has occurred. He is not concerned with any of this - indeed, his job is to strip away the context and reduce a problem to its bare essentials. Once solved, or a compromise enforced by a court of law, the whole system moves on to the next dispute somewhere else.

Lawyers think in the short term. It's part of the job. They are trained to be pragmatic, get a problem out of the way and move quickly on to the next one. Lawyers are practically prohibited from seeing the larger picture, from considering the consequences tomorrow of the actions and decisions they enforce today. Most importantly, they are reminded daily, hourly, that they are *not responsible*. All they are required to do is enact the processes of law. There's not to reason why, merely to get a result. Because of this, lawyers are functionaries not visionaries, pragmatists not philosophers, tacticians not strategists.

Why does this matter? It wouldn't if lawyers remained doing the job they started out to do, namely, to deal with particular difficulties in situations where their services were sought and paid for as a last resort. But this is no longer the case. Today lawyers are being asked to frame the very structure of our lives, not only of individuals but of nations and states.

Why? Look at the government. What do you see? A row of lawyers. At the last count, two thirds of the cabinet were trained (with few practising) lawyers. The Prime Minister is a lawyer, the Chancellor of the Exchequer, too. That's the two most powerful men in politics. Men whose very training has been to take each situation as it arises, argue the toss, win or lose, and move on. When they run out of ideas themselves, who are they likely to turn to? Other lawyers, of course. Isn't this precisely what we are seeing? Great debaters, yes, very good at getting their own way, but is this the mindset we need to govern a country?

Why are lawyers so attracted to politics? Certainly, politicians need some of the qualities lawyers possess. But they need an awful lot more besides. Once government is reduced to people shouting and bullying each other to get their own way, or to get re-elected, it is debased beyond reason. Secondly, to be truly successful, as well as being true to themselves, politicians need to be able to see ahead, to have a plan, a vision for the future. This ability comes easily to relatively few people. Those who don't have it, don't even understand what it is. When George Bush Snr asked: "What is this vision thing?" he wasn't joking. He was admitting he didn't know.

Lawyers by and large don't have vision, not as fully-grown adults anyway. They may have had it once, but if so, it will have been knocked out of them long ago. Somebody once said that every child is a natural salesman. Try refusing to buy a child an ice-cream if you don't believe that. Where have all the salesmen gone by the time they are twenty-one? The same thing happens to visionaries, their parents tell them to stop 'dreaming' and get on with the things that matter, like getting a job.

Writers, painters, artists have vision. Winston Churchill was all of these. Scientists have vision. Margaret Thatcher was a scientist. Tony Blair was a lawyer.

I know some very nice lawyers, one of my closest friends is one. He was never tempted to be a politician. He knows his limitations. In fact, like all good lawyers, he spends most of his time trying to stop people resorting to the law. He has a healthy distrust of barristers, courts, juries and judges, as we all should. I have two other lawyer friends, one of whom retired last year and the other is just about to. Both of them say they hated their jobs and are decidedly happy to be out of the profession. At the same time I see a huge number of kids, especially girls, desperate to get in. What's going on? This can't all be down to Ally McBeal and Jenny Seagrove, can it?

I tell you, going into the law may seem sophisticated and rewarding, but I'd rather do almost anything else any day.

Meanwhile, surely we can dredge up a few more candidates from the ranks of the non-lawyers to run the country.

Please.

"Woe unto you, lawyers, for you have taken away the key of knowledge!"

THE BIBLE

The Nanny State

People who take pride in self-reliance deplore the encroachment of the state into their homes and private lives. They also think we're breeding a new generation which has lost the ability to think for itself. Losing the freedom to control your own destiny is a big price to pay for an occasional helping hand from Big Brother.

MOST of us don't like other people thinking they know what's best for us.

Personally I prefer to think that the job of an elected government is to help and assist me achieve my reasonable goals and expectations, as long as I'm not hurting anyone else, and to provide me with a relatively safe environment in which to do so - which I am happy to pay for. I don't expect the government to tell me what those goals and expectations should be. In theory, at any rate, politicians are there to serve us. In practice, as we are learning to our cost, it can too easily end up the other way around.

For democracy to work – in other words for our elected representatives to actually represent us – the views of the majority must prevail. How can it work any other way? Presuming, of course, that we have a 'majority' in the first place. I think we still have, it's just harder to find it. Despite society becoming more and more diversified, with politicians and media magnifying our differences and a growing number of 'minorities' only too ready to promote their own agendas, nevertheless, I still believe we overwhelmingly share a desire for freedom, decency and generosity of spirit.

We may have lost sight of what most people want, but that doesn't mean a consensus no longer exists.

Until our political parties recognise this and bring it to the forefront of their thinking they are stymied. Short of holding a referendum on every issue of any significance (not a bad idea but one that successive governments have rejected) our increasingly out-dated, two and a half party system will not only fail to come up with the answers, it won't even know the questions.

So, what to do? In the circumstances you might presume as little as possible - just let people get on with their lives and see how it all shakes out. What we actually have is precisely the opposite, namely, a small elite running the country who, having completely lost touch with what people want, meet from time to time behind closed doors, decide what's best for the rest of us and get on with enforcing it. Regardless.

As a matter of fact, it's worse than that. For a long time we have had a vainglorious, lame-duck Prime Minister desperate to be remembered for anything other than leading us into an illegal and ill-fated war, announcing one populist, right-of-centre initiative after another, only to be thwarted by his left-of-centre colleagues, particularly his next door neighbour and would-be successor. At the same time, there is the relentless implementation of an old-style, left-wing 'reforming' agenda, no longer robbing the rich to pay the poor but to finance the burgeoning public sector necessary to force through its bigoted, outdated ideas.

In short, we have a surplus of the manure required to fertilise the shoots of a Nanny State.

The idea that people should be 'good citizens' first and foremost, indoctrinated from cradle to grave, rewarded for their loyalty to the state and its ideas and punished for their transgressions is nothing new. Except we've never had it here. In China, yes, and throughout the length and breadth of the former Soviet Republic, even in Germany under the Third Reich, but never here.

And yet, Nanny can be quite seductive.

Most of us are lazy at heart. Why stand when Nanny will pull you up a chair or sit when she'll tuck you up in bed? Why take responsibility for your life when Nanny will look after you? All you have to do is agree with everything she says and, in return, Nanny will take all your worries away, provide you with a livelihood, educate your children, look after you when you are ill, even give you a roof over your head. Providing you do as you are told. You can't have it both ways. That's the deal. Once you've signed up with Nanny you forfeit independence of thought, freedom of speech, your right to parent your children, to plan your career, to decide where you live... the list goes on. Sounds crazy, doesn't it, but you don't have to look too hard to see the warning signs now.

Already we have dodgy political ideology being taught in schools, government interference in the once sacrosanct areas of marriage and family life, huge rafts of legislation governing relationships between employers and employees, health and safety, pollution, blatant social engineering - most importantly but not solely in education - intolerable levels of regulation in commerce and industry, not to mention the unprecedented extent of the invasion of individual privacy by the state through the introduction of identity cards, DNA sampling and CCTV cameras on every street corner. Add to this the changing attitudes and busy-bodying of the police, sadly no longer the first port-of-call for anyone in trouble but rather the enforcers of state-sponsored political correctness, as well as nearly a quarter of the working population employed by the state (and rising) and you have the obvious and clear blueprint for what could so easily follow. Unless, somehow, this madness can be halted.

It is astonishing that this should be happening here. Certainly those generations born since the war have led an incredibly sheltered existence. Obviously we have forgotten the hundreds of thousands of youngsters killed in two world wars to preserve the very freedoms we now seem so ready to give up. Without doubt we have become complacent, no longer able to comprehend how our precious way of life, so meticulously constructed over such a long period of time at such great cost, can be dismantled so quickly, and once destroyed, be lost forever.

The Nanny State may seem an attractive option for a population already bloated by affluence, rendered idle by lack of necessity and cocooned in a mythical sense of security. Unfortunately, the more we expect the state to look after us, the more we surrender the things that really matter to us as human beings.

When communism finally imploded in Russia, the celebrations quickly gave way to self-doubt and insecurity as the millions freed from the oppression of an all-controlling communist regime quickly discovered they had lost the ability to fend for themselves.

Happily we are nowhere near that point yet. But, as the checks and balances built into our unwritten and vulnerable constitution are systematically removed, there remains the danger that we could end up with something very much like it. Except, in our case, we will arrive there by default rather than revolution.

Keep a watchful eye on the progress of the Nanny State.

"There is no greater threat to the people of this planet than the retreat from reason we see all around us today."

LORD LAWSON

Charity

Taxi drivers in general are a well-meaning bunch, happy to give
their services free once in a while whether ferrying disabled
kids to the seaside or organising outings for OAPs. But, in
today's complex society, 'charity' is not as simple as that. The
question is what does it actually mean in the 21st century?

THERE are 150,000 charities registered in the UK - and an
awful lot more that aren't. All of them collect money from Joe
Public and 're-direct' it to those they say are in need. With
a total gross income of over £20billion, Robin Hood would
be proud. Or would he?

As things stand anyone can set up a charity providing
they can come up with a convincing reason to ask for your
money. Whether you should give it or not is another matter
– they might just use it to pay themselves generous expenses
or, in extreme cases, a handsome salary! They might even
work on the basis that so long as something, however little,
is left over at the end of the year for the original cause, that's
good enough. But, is it?

Registered charities are supposed to account to the
Charity Commission, a body which costs the taxpayer more
than £30m a year and, by its own admission, believes in
letting the trustees of charities get on with their job with as
little interference as possible. This provides the big charities

with big opportunities. For example, they can decide that it is in 'their best interests' to spend millions on advertising, even though the advertising is being paid for with money that has been donated for an entirely different purpose! Let me ask you: would you give money to a charity knowing they were going to spend it on advertising? Or, at the very least, shouldn't they tell you that to start with? Have you ever seen a charity advertisement which says "donations received from this advertisement will be used to pay for this advertisement,"? I'm all for relaxing regulation rather than increasing it, but the charity industry could just be the exception that proves the rule.

Let's be more specific. If you knew that a major children's charity was collecting over £30m a year and spending £25m on costs and overheads, how would you react? Would you say 'great, that's £5m the kids wouldn't otherwise get' or 'sorry, I really don't want my money being used to pay for a huge wage bill, let alone a multi-million pound marketing campaign.'

Would you believe that in the last two years at least one major charity went broke? Not because it gave too much away, but because it overspent on purchases and administration. Don't worry, it's had a 're-birth' and is still going strong.

If you think these cases are imaginary, they're not and there's plenty more of them out there. They know who they are.

No, it is simply not right for charities to set themselves up as commercial operations with highly paid CEO's and senior management, expense accounts, company cars, moving expenses, pensions, private health insurance (not to mention all the other perks highly paid executives expect) merely for the little that's left to be spent on the thing you thought you were supporting in the first place!

Now, I'm not saying there isn't another side to all this. Happily there are plenty of proper charities out there doing a good job, keeping their overheads low, maintaining a high level of voluntary involvement (so that not everyone working for the charity is a paid employee) and, in those cases where large sums are spent on staff, employing people who are actually providing real help and assistance to those in need. Such charities are able to submit annual sets of accounts which make for re-assuring reading.

Needless to say government is in on the act, keen to encourage the charity sector to save them money! Ironically, in an age when our political leaders boast of the state's ever increasing support for those in need, so it expects the charity sector to provide a bigger than ever contribution. Put another way it means that at a time when total revenue from taxation has never been higher, we are being asked to give away even more on top. Of course, the Chancellor could do more to encourage us, but, beyond the modest benefits of Gift Aid (which only applies to individuals and not companies) he won't.

Which raises a crucial point, namely, why do people give to charity at all?

The United Kingdom, or rather its population, has a long tradition of being charitable. In fact, compared to just about everywhere else, including the US, we are the most charitable nation in the world. Much of this derives from our Christian tradition as well as the fact that most of us like to feel unselfish from time to time. Helping the less fortunate carries with it a 'feel-good factor' totally missing from the legal requirement to pay tax. When did you last get a warm glow from paying a cheque to the Inland Revenue? Nevertheless, I've heard the question asked often enough:

why we should be expected to support charities when we already pay through the nose for a perfectly adequate welfare state?

Well, to start with, the welfare state is far from adequate. Ask anyone who has tried to get a wheelchair or a bath lift or a specially adapted coach for the disabled and you'll hear of appalling inefficiency, incompetence and lack of funding. Appeal to the right charity, however, and you're likely to get a refreshingly immediate, individually tailored response. The Variety Club, one of my favourites, and one of the oldest children's charities in the world, still manages to supply a whole range of special needs equipment – including coaches and wheelchairs - faster, more cheaply and with a fraction of the hassle encountered from local authorities. The evidence is in the demand. There is simply no sign of appeals to charities drying up, despite increased funding year-on-year on social services. In fact, quite the reverse.

Even if the state system was to get its act together, there would still be a need for charity, if only because there will always be those who want to give something back, particularly those who feel life has been kind to them. Companies, too, appear to be developing a charitable conscience and, increasingly, balance sheets reflect the need for them to contribute to the community in which they operate.

So, if giving to charity is on your agenda, how can you make sure your money will be well spent? Which charity should you support because, let's face it, you have a huge choice? It all depends on how serious you are. Of course, it's fine to give your money away without too much thought, maybe because you have been moved by an appeal on television, or on the radio or at some charity function. But this is only the half of it. If you are actually interested in helping the end user rather than just getting a buzz out of giving, then you probably need to delve a little deeper. Here are some useful questions to ask:

(1) Are the charity's objectives realistic and achievable? For example, I have always had a problem with claims such as 'Let's stamp out cruelty to children.' A worthy and emotive cause indeed, but how the hell are you going to do it, bearing in mind that 90% of child cruelty happens in secrecy behind closed doors, out of sight of the do-gooders, however well-intentioned they may be? You may, of course, take a different view but the question remains.

(2) Do you want your money to be spent here or overseas? If you don't mind that's okay, but, remember, a huge chunk of the money sent to developing countries still gets 'lost' before it arrives at its final destination. If it arrives at all.

(3) Are you concerned about the percentage of your donation that goes to the charity's own overheads and staff costs? You can make up your own mind but only if you know the facts.

(4) Are you giving your money to a 'real' charity at all, specifically, a charity supported and run by volunteers giving their time freely without recompense, or is it a business registered as a charity with only its surplus 'profits', if any, benefiting the community?

You are entitled to know the answers to these and as many other questions as you like before you give your cash away. How do you find out? Ask. You'll be surprised how quickly you can scare off an over-persistent fundraiser by requesting a set of the charity's accounts. If you get them you'll learn a lot about that charity. If you don't, forget it. Try the internet, too.

Taking the helicopter view, the picture's still mainly good. But in this age of everyone from big business to government jumping on the band wagon, keep an eye on the charity sector. It could go one of two ways: either charities will start gobbling each other up and we'll end up with far fewer but more powerful 'commercial' charities, not dissimilar to big companies, who will re-define the nature of charitable giving to suit themselves - or, it could go the other way with lots of smaller, unaccountable outfits cropping up all over the place with dubious objectives and practices whose main objective is to provide a livelihood for the people running them. It's a volatile business which, by definition, depends upon exploiting people's kindness and generosity.

Just make sure you don't get hurt in the process.

P.S. It annoys me when you're on holiday in some faraway place and the tour rep tells you not to give your loose change to beggars because it only 'encourages' them. Why shouldn't they be encouraged? Yes, there's the risk that some of them are obtaining money under false pretences, but since you're only talking about less than the price of a packet of fags, isn't it worth the risk for a clear conscience? Or is it that we'd prefer not to be pestered, not to have to stare poverty in the face? When you're staying in posh hotels, spending obscene amounts of money on food and drink, it's uncomfortable to be reminded that someone else could live for a month on your daily bar bill. Better to close your eyes and hope they'll go away. Or send a donation through a nice charity back home who will do the dirty work for you.

Personally, I'd rather see the smile on a beggar's face – even if I am being ripped off.

Gordon Brown collected £22.5billion of income tax in January 2007, the largest amount since record began and double the amount of revenue compared with when he was first Chancellor - without ever announcing an increase in income tax.

TREASURY FIGURES

Bureaucracy

Most taxi drivers are self-employed and acutely aware of the necessity to make ends meet. Taxation is a naturally contentious subject and one that is aired with increasing frequency as spending by the state gets further and further out of control.

HERE'S a thought. Have you ever stopped to wonder why we've got more and more people working in Westminster when nearly three-quarters of our laws - plus large chunks of our lives - are now being master-minded in Brussels?

Surely, one of the few benefits that might have come from the centralisation of power within a single European parliament would have been some significant cost savings here. Needless to say, the reverse has been the case.

If you had any doubt about the increasing intervention of government in our lives, take a closer look at the devolution of power. Far from these incredibly costly new 'assemblies' - not only in Brussels but also in Wales and Scotland - replacing a single overburdened central administration, they have been layered on top of it! Result? A hugely expanded governing class.

It's an extraordinary phenomenon that the less of a job there is to be done, the more people get employed to do it. Not in accountable organisations, of course. If a commercial firm were to be run in this way it would plunge into loss and go bankrupt very quickly indeed. Customers would simply refuse to stomach the higher and higher prices it would need to charge to cover its increasing overheads. But with government, as costs mount, all you have to do is pass it on in the form of increased taxes to your customers and, regardless of their views on the matter, enforce your demands by law.

There's no need to worry about efficiency or cost effectiveness when you have the law on your side. Just go on fleecing the man in the street. He'll pay for your incompetence and mismanagement and, if he won't or can't, he goes to prison, not you. In any other walk of life we'd call this extortion.

In the la-la land of bureaucracy it's called taxation.

"Interference, constant imposition of initiatives and ever-growing bureaucratic demands must be ended."
STEVE SINNOTI, GENERAL SECRETARY OF THE NUT

The Environment

One minute he'll lecture you on how the weather's changed
since he was a kid, the next he'll admit to polluting the
atmosphere - but your cabby is not halfway to being
convinced there's any connection between the two.

IT seems as if the 'Green Lobby' has finally got its way.

First they tried dolphins, whales and the rain forests and a fat lot of good it did them. Then they hit on aerosols making holes in space, which managed to raise an eyebrow or two. Most recently, throwing caution to the winds and in a last ditch attempt to get taken seriously, their latest 'coup de grace' seems to have worked. Namely, that we are destroying the planet. Actually destroying it.

Well, it's done the trick. This time we've sat up and taken notice. Now The Environment is the hot topic – climate change, greenhouse gases, holes in the ozone layer, ice caps melting, de-forestation, etc, etc. And why is all this occurring? Never mind that these changes have all happened before as the Sun and the Earth follow their natural cycle, this time its because 'we', that is the wicked capitalists of the west, have not been taking care of our planet.

Of course, in today's politik-speak, the 'we' means fat cat businessmen, industrialists, banks, aviation and oil companies, car manufacturers, the pharmaceutical and chemical giants, not to mention that sales director's missus down the road who takes her kids to school in a Korean four-by-four. No wonder then that politicians are jumping on to what they see as a sure-fire vote winner - that those who are rich must be evil, so evil, in fact, that they are destroying the very planet we live on. So, out it comes again, that tired, dog-eared old 'them-and-us' dogma, salvaged from the leftist loft, dusted down and tossed at us in its latest eco-friendly form:

The rich are destroying the world.

I don't buy it, not at all.

You see it is exactly these people, engaged in a variety of generally productive and useful activities, we should be thanking for the way of life we enjoy today. And which, lest we forget, is the envy of the so-called 'under-developed' countries who, whether we like it or not, can't wait to grab a bit of our corrupt western lifestyle for themselves. Can you imagine what it will be like when China and India are industrialised like us? India alone, with a population of over a billion is well on its way, China's not far behind and South America and Africa haven't even got off the blocks.

Of course, even the politicians have to accept that whatever we do in the UK is not going to make a scrap of difference. So, we are being told that we have to make dramatic changes in our daily lives in order to 'set an example' to the rest of the world. Well, I ask you! Do you think the Chinese will take a blind bit of notice of us, who they perceive as having enjoyed a way of life they couldn't even have imagined for the last century, telling them what they should or shouldn't do? That's not just because we are a tiny country, either, their reaction to the Americans would be even more dismissive. Let's face it, these sleeping giants are going to be burning fossil fuels and releasing CFC's into the atmosphere like there's no tomorrow in pursuit of exactly the same things that we take for granted. Talk about hard cheese. Talk about shutting the gate after the horse has bolted.

No, what *will* happen is that European governments, so keen to get a stronger and stricter grasp over their inconveniently disobedient electorates, will play the environmental card for as long as it suits them to do so - incidentally, raising billions more revenue in the process through taxing 'anti-green' practices. For the time being, it's an easy trick to pull simply because, unlike politicians by and large, the public does have a conscience, which is greatly to its credit.

Strangely enough, if the green issues had been presented against a backdrop of a less sensationalised, smaller domestic agenda, it might have been easier to go along with. Like most people, I don't like smoke, fumes, polluted rivers, filthy coastlines, chemicals in my drinking water, over-crowding or excessive noise. Ironically – and not entirely surprisingly – most of these things have got worse rather than better whilst the politicians have been twittering on about the future of mankind.

Here's a final thought. If the world is to continue to industrialise, as it will to an unprecedented degree and at a pace we can hardly envisage, and if we prohibit or drastically cut down on the use of fossil fuels, what will be the energy source that replaces them?

There is only one answer: nuclear power, again on a scale we have never allowed ourselves to imagine. Cast your mind back. What was it we were all so terrified of twenty, thirty years ago? Nuclear waste. The stuff you can't get rid of, that remains deadly dangerous for a hundred years (maybe longer, how can we know?), that has to be transported, buried in concrete containers and then maintained at immense cost to ensure its safety. Not to mention the fact that governments of all 'environmentally responsible' third-world nations will, as a matter of course, demand the right to a nuclear capability - to generate power, of course. It's already happening and we all know where it could lead.

So, there's the irony. That, in their quest to save the planet from the adverse effects of burning fossil fuels, the 'eco-friendlies', aided and abetted by the guardians of our nanny superstate, will finally unleash the most horrifying and destructive force of all.

Now, that's something that *could* destroy the world.

"The Government has withheld vital information on the costs of new nuclear plants and the disposal of radioactive waste...their approach has been misleading, seriously flawed and procedurally unfair."

MR JUSTICE SULLIVAN'S RULING IN A HIGH COURT
JUDICIAL REVIEW, FEBRUARY 2007

War

The driver who picked me up at Admiralty Arch had been talking to a senior army officer who complained that, despite increased overseas military commitments, the strength of our Armed Services was cut from 217,000 to 210,000 last year. One thing led to another...

NOBODY knows whether wars are inevitable but all the evidence would suggest that we're stuck with them for a while yet. As long as we have wildly differing views as to how we want the world to be, there will always be a small minority of people who, driven by greed, power, self-righteousness or good old religious fanaticism, will see war as the only possible way to get there. Their way.

The trouble is that despite, maybe because of, the vast arsenals of weaponry and military power available to today's protagonists, war simply ain't what it used to be.

Now, with the threat of wide scale nuclear destruction receding (more on this later), the sort of wars we used to have are no longer there to be fought. The reason? Because those wars, where killing as many people as possible and reducing a country to rubble in the process - to be subsequently rebuilt by the victorious invader - no longer achieve a goal anyone wants. It was easy for Kitchener - or Churchill, for that matter - to say that the side which caused most casualties would inevitably win, because (a) human life was much cheaper then and (b) no-one was counting the cost of re-building the defeated country.

Technically we may have won the 2nd World War but it broke us in the process and, more than half a century later, we have not recovered. A moral victory, if there is such a thing, yes, but in every other sense a disaster. Far from protecting the much-coveted English/British way of life, it changed it out of all recognition.

In fact, we still hadn't got over the 1st World War, only twenty-five years earlier, which cost us a whole generation in order to win. The ramifications are still with us, not least the flawed policy of planned immigration, no less than a crude attempt by the political classes who led us into these wars in the first place, to replace the millions of youngsters we lost.

Lessons are sometimes learnt and it is indeed unthinkable today that any western government would make these same mistakes again, even if the public were prepared to act as cannon-fodder, which it isn't. Yet, war still persists.

Of course, one of the things that two massive wars spawned was a highly profitable arms industry, which, by definition, has found it hard to sustain itself without the odd skirmish. Arms dealers run businesses and businesses need customers so, not surprisingly, if the domestic market dries up, others have to be found further afield.

Two things have happened here. For many years after the war, principally in Europe and America, governments were persuaded that the only guarantee of peace was to build up huge arsenals of more and more sophisticated weaponry to act as a deterrent to anyone who might otherwise think of attacking you - the so-called 'cold' war. Amazingly and encouragingly, a very small group of world leaders (including Margaret Thatcher) exploded this myth in the eighties and, coupled with the disintegration of the Soviet power block, widespread disarmament began in earnest. Needless to say, this drove the arms dealers further east to find pastures new. Consequently, we now have both east and west stacked up with modern conventional weaponry most of which is quite useless in fighting the sort of wars we are confronted with today.

Yesterday's wars were fought by huge armies causing huge casualties. Although none of the great generals were beyond a bit of cheating, nonetheless wars were largely 'public school' affairs with rules and regulations, and a sense of fair play on both sides. Doesn't seem possible in hindsight, does it, but ask those involved and they will tell you stories of British and German soldiers declaring a truce on Christmas Day and singing carols together. There were international conventions and agreements, for example, on surrender and the treatment of prisoners, which both sides were expected to abide by and largely did. Everyone knew what a war crime was - and all of this amidst the horror and carnage of the bloodiest confrontations in our history.

Those were wars of country against country, whole populations waging war against each other, united behind their 'front lines' in acts of virtually united patriotism. How likely is it that such wars will ever be fought again?

Compare them with the wars of today, the 'war' in Iraq, for example, although we could just as easily take Vietnam, Afghanistan, Bosnia, even Northern Ireland, any of them. What's changed? I'll tell you. *The losers won't lose. They won't lie down and die.*

Here's how it goes. Phase one - the 'good' guys go in with their superior military might and obliterate the opposition. Usually this doesn't take very long, very few people are hurt and within hours the conquerors are marching victoriously through the streets. So far, so good. Then, phase two – the international media descend on the 'good guys' questioning the morality of such a victory, indeed, questioning whether there has been a victory at all. Phase three – the conquering heroes begin the process of trying to establish law and order in the wake of the chaos they have caused although, strangely, life seems to be going on much as before. Phase four – the victorious army comes under attack from seemingly disorganised guerrilla forces who seem to appear from nowhere and disappear just as mysteriously. For want of better words these shadowy forces are named 'insurgents' and/or 'terrorists' although, rather like the French resistance in WW2, all they are doing is continuing to fight against the invading army. Phase five – the occupying forces find that conventional methods of war are hopeless in combating this type of sporadic but sustained attack and become dispirited and demoralised. Phase six – frustrated and disillusioned, and aided by demands for withdrawal from back home, the victorious army retreats leaving local police and local politicians to clear up the mess.

This is a new world. Anyone can get a few crates of machine guns and a grenade or two. The enemy doesn't have to give up and certainly won't surrender. There are no rules of engagement and any sort of moral stance is demolished once the media tears into it. What's more, no democratic government can hold firm for long once it has lost the support of an increasingly multi-cultural and divided electorate.

And yet wars won't go away. So, what to do?

The root of the problem is that we're still trying to fight them the way they were fought a hundred years ago. Encouraged by over-zealous politicians who, feeling increasingly impotent domestically, can only seek glory on the world stage - and who are themselves in league with powerful arms dealers exhorting us to stick to conventional methods of war so they can sell us billions of pounds worth of weapons - we are treating political and commercial skirmishes as if they were WW2. What we need to do is find a new way to fight *amongst* the people and not *against* them.

What does this mean in real terms? It comes back to the nuclear alternative. The only-to-be-imagined horror of a world-scale nuclear annihilation has shocked us all into realising that wars by people against people are no longer an option. *This* is the modern equivalent of World War 2, *not* the wars in Iraq or Afghanistan or Cambodia. The hydrogen bomb is the ultimate end to which mass conventional war theory has led. We didn't like it and so far, thank God, we haven't used it in the last sixty years. But with the abandonment of the nuclear option, so must we abandon the idea that there is some other sort of scaled-down conventional strategy available to us. There isn't. Just a vacuum where conventional warfare once was. Any attempt to win a conventional war, assuming only that the protagonists have the resolve to see it through to the bitter end, must inevitably result in the use of the nuclear option. That's what ended World War Two and it would happen again. Therefore, if we are rejecting the nuclear option out of hand, we must reject any attempt to fight a war using conventional methods.

You can only fight a bully by being a bully. You can only fight a terrorist by becoming one yourself. Not a nice thought but, in the end, it has a nightmarish logic. Modern warfare is synonymous with terrorism. Therefore we have to train terrorists who are better than the terrorists we are fighting. If Osama Bin Laden can set up terrorist training camps then we have to do the same. Then we have to revise our conventions and rules of engagement to make way for this new, insidious form of conflict. Ask the Israelis, they know.

Soon, we shall have to start fighting the modern enemy in a way he understands.

The sooner, the better.

"If any question why we died
tell them because our fathers lied."
RUDYARD KIPLING

Creativity

Most taxi drivers seem reasonably happy with their lot - apart from at airports where they appear to have flown in from a different planet. Contentment requires imagination, however, and the job seems to provide plenty of scope for exercising it.

IMAGINE a street, a crescent of houses, with the familiar litter and rubbish of suburban life strewn about, in the gutters, in the alleys between the houses, around the gateposts and garage doors. It is 8.30am on a Monday morning. A road sweeper turns up. His job is to clear up the street, take what he has swept up to the council tip and get back to his depot by noon. He stands for a minute looking at the task ahead, picturing how pleasant the crescent would look devoid of the cigarette packets, the burger box, the discarded cellophane wrapping, the tissue, the half-shredded newspaper. He looks at his watch. Three hours should do it and the crescent will look as good as new. By eleven-thirty the street is clear, the rubbish is in his cart. The street looks just the way he thought it would before he started. He sets off back to the depot.

The following week a different road sweeper arrives. Same time, same place. He sees the rubbish and starts clearing it away. At eleven-thirty the job is done and he's on his way back to the depot.

The result is identical - the residents have a clean street achieved in exactly the same time using the same equipment. So, what's the difference? Here's the answer: the first road sweeper got some real satisfaction from doing his job. The second one just got paid for it.

Of course, to understand this, you have to be able to imagine the situation for yourself. If you can't, you are probably suffering from an imagination deficiency, too, so there's not much point in reading on.

The neat thing about that story is that the only person who benefits from using his imagination is the road sweeper himself. In other instances, a whole lot of other people benefit, too. To appreciate this fully you need to realise that pretty well every film, TV programme, book, record, building, painting, piece of furniture, car – you name it – has started life as a blank sheet of paper. To put something onto that piece of paper (or computer screen) requires the supreme act of applying God's greatest gift to man, namely, the imagination.

For 'imagination' substitute 'creativity' – you can't have one without the other. However, it's perfectly possible to have neither. Think about the people you know. How much evidence of creativity or imagination do you see? Not a lot. Yet so much of what we take for granted comes from the efforts and imagination of a very small number of people. Someone, somewhere has used his or her imagination to remarkable effect. The rest of us feel re-invigorated, encouraged, optimistic, happy even, simply because something – anything – has been magically created or simply elevated from the bog standard to the special.

Visiting a hospital the other day I was pleasantly surprised to see that the children's ward had been beautifully decorated with simple, inexpensive murals. Judging by other hospitals I've been to, this was certainly not the norm and was surprisingly uplifting. It would be nice to think of lots more examples.

I have come to believe that we humans are not divided by class, education, wealth or culture but by our ability or otherwise to use our imagination. People either have it or they don't and there's not a lot in between. By and large society divides into two groups, 'creatives' and 'non-creatives', each finding it difficult to understand the other. The trouble is those who don't have it can't imagine what it's like for the ones who do!

It's easy to see why the non-creative majority regards the creative minority with suspicion. Ironic, really, when you think how much those few enrich our lives. The problem is that the nature of the creative mind is to be inconvenient, questioning, impatient, even rebellious. Which makes it risky to include such people on committees and quangos, in boardrooms and, well, frankly, almost any of the bodies and institutions that run our lives. What's worse, they have an irritating habit of seeming to be out of step with the prevailing view. Back to the 'spirit of contradiction'!

Nevertheless, we allow them their place – providing they stay there. Moreover, we're prepared to pay them handsomely to make sure they do. Musicians, entertainers, writers, artists of all kinds can and do earn fortunes. Try paying a tenth of what Elton John makes to the chairman of a public company and you'll have a riot on your hands. Why? Because Elton can do something that no businessman can. He can make you happy, make you sad, make you laugh, make you cry. That's worth whatever it costs and the laws of supply and demand apply. What's more, we want him to go on doing it! Not to get distracted by other things, like putting the world to rights. Sir Bob Geldorf tried that and gave up all hope of ever being taken seriously as an artist again. Plus, if we pay our creatives enough they won't be able to afford to take on the lowly paid, if very much more powerful jobs, in management or politics. The non-creatives will always end up ruling because, in the end, there are simply more of them.

Here's another thing about creative people. They are not as concerned about a secure lifestyle as the rest of us. Not simply because they can earn big money, but because they know they can rely on their imagination, their inventiveness, when the need arises. Because they can do something that others can't, they are in demand. Which is why so many end up living what may seem to be insecure and uncertain lives. This is where your freelancers and self-employed come from – and, make no mistake about it, being a plasterer, decorator, landscape gardener, a kitchen designer or a builder is every bit as creative as writing songs and painting pictures. You see, this is using the word 'creative' in its broadest sense. When we talk about creative people 'not fitting in', it is not because they are eccentric, it's because they don't need the trappings of employment to make them feel safe. So, if the rest of us are reluctant to let them get too involved in the mainstream of things, very often they are only too happy to oblige.

What else makes us suspicious of creative people? Well, for one thing they're few and far between and we are always scared of those who are 'different'. For another, there is a widespread lack of insight as to how creative people function and go about things. Instead, creativity is perceived as a gift or just good fortune, in other words, 'luck'. "Aren't you lucky to be able to play the piano?" I've been told all my life. "Yes", I reply, knowing that if I tried to explain the number of hours I'd practised, the obsession to get it right, the sacrifices along the way, the pride and self-respect that were at stake, even as a child... am I losing you, yet? They'd never believe me, either, or I'd be written off as a nutcase. It's easier to say: "Yeah, I was lucky, you're right."

Let's go on using 'creative' in the broadest sense. In fact, let's not just talk about those who are obviously creative, those who wear their creativity on their sleeve. Creativity goes far beyond 'artistry' and 'invention'. I know a number of unmistakably creative people who can't sing, write or draw. Or who have never tried to, or wanted to. I remember Steffi Graf, possibly the greatest women's tennis player of all time, once saying that, despite her achievements, she was probably not the most *talented* player in the world, that there were almost certainly more talented players than her, it was just that they were working as lawyers, secretaries or nurses while she'd stuck to tennis. Who knows how successful my apparently non-creative friends would have been had they taken up composing, painting or writing? They didn't. Instead they went into other walks of life where their innate creativity reaped them different rewards and where other creative people were drawn to them like moths to a lamp recognising a soul mate even if they may not have appeared as overtly creative as themselves.

It appears that truly creative people have a fundamentally different approach to the world. It comes back to the imagination. Babies and children all seem to have it at birth but in most it is quickly extinguished. Only in a few does it go on to flourish for the rest of life. It's easy to recognise in storytelling, painting, composing, dancing – and so on. What is less obvious is that the same power of imagination can affect everything we do. It doesn't matter whether you are writing a play or filling in a VAT return. If you can imagine the finished result the job becomes simpler and much more enjoyable.

Let's go back to our road sweeper. The man who can visualise a beautifully clean street is not only motivated to get on with what is a basically tedious job, but will work more happily to that end encouraged by the prospect of seeing his mental picture become reality. Compare this with the non-creative approach – all this man knows is that he has to collect rubbish, piece by piece, and put it in the receptacle provided. He achieves the same result but gets little or no fulfilment or satisfaction from doing so. You might ask whether it is possible to have a creative approach to sweeping a road? Yes, and a few road sweepers will have it.

Of course, you don't have to have imagination to set yourself objectives. I know a number of highly ambitious men and women with no imagination at all. The trouble is, they invariably choose the wrong objectives. Take young people who are ambitious to make money, we've all met them. "By the time I'm thirty," they say, "I'm going to be a millionaire!" It never works. The wealthy people I know have achieved it as a by-product of pursuing some other goal, usually something they love doing. Nick Faldo doesn't continue playing golf to make money, nor is that the reason Rupert Murdoch goes into the office every day. These men are inspired by dreams. And dreams are the stuff of the imagination.

All of this is relevant as we move towards a new kind of economy. The internet and its associated technology has created new business opportunities requiring a different kind of commercial mindset. Gone are the days of protecting ones ideas and inventions. In today's new world, the new breed of young 'serial entrepreneurs' know that it is by sharing their ideas and making them freely available to others that they will ultimately reap their rewards. We are already seeing signs that the consumer-led economy of the second half of the last century, which in turn replaced the manufacturing economy, is itself being replaced by what we might call the 'creator economy'. And, if this trend continues, as seems likely, we are going to need creative people as never before.

Without the ability to harness the power of the imagination, man is failing to fulfil his destiny, just as surely as if he were missing the power of sight, smell or taste. He cannot know what it is like for others to be imaginative and creative because he has never felt it in himself. In this state man is a lesser creature, reduced to making the best of life on a day-to-day basis, dealing with problems as they arise believing that the future he can't envisage will take care of itself. If we allow people like this to become our leaders, to run our lives, we will sense a terrible void, a vacuum, where the driving force of the imagination should be. Something essential in the soul and spirit of men and women will be lacking and the consequences grave.

Creative people leave their mark on history even when they were wrong - Churchill, Luther King, Mandela, Henry Ford, Barnes Wallis, Shakespeare, Walt Disney, H.G.Wells, even Margaret Thatcher. The others don't. It may not be fair but creativity, the ability to harness the incredible power of the imagination, is the unmistakable ingredient of greatness. Those who lack it must learn to recognise it in others and move aside to let them bloom and blossom. Only then will our industries, institutions and communities blossom, too.

If we want mankind to fare better than our fellow earthly inhabitants, we must find a way to promote rather than suppress the greatest single quality that distinguishes us from them. Our imagination.

> *"One can exist without art, but one cannot live without it."*
>
> OSCAR WILDE (although not one of his best)

Kids

*I often wonder what other people think when they see
me in a restaurant with a beautiful young woman - they
won't assume she's my daughter, I bet. Taxi drivers love
a wink and a nod. We all love our kids but it's easier
than you might imagine to take them for granted.*

LOVE 'em or hate 'em, they're not going to go away, so
perhaps we might give them a teeny-weeny bit more thought
than we do.

Let's start with discipline – funny how contentious that
word sounds nowadays, isn't it? When I was a kid it was the
word you heard most often when people talked about bringing
up children. Nowadays, we tend to think that discipline is a
thing of the past. More than that, we are coming very close
to the point of believing it's bad and those who attempt to
administer it are very bad indeed. Is this right?

It really comes down to the age-old principle of
punishment and reward, yet even the word 'punishment' feels
uneasy. It seems so out of touch with the spirit of our times.
When we are reluctant even to punish criminals, people
who have actually hurt others, how can we even think about
punishing a child?

There are a lot of factors here, not least an increasing
awareness that when someone is punished, there has to be

someone else to administer the punishment; the implication being that one of the parties is better, more virtuous and morally superior to the other. Generally, we've gone off this idea, although, not so long ago, it was the bedrock upon which the order of our society was built. Men and women would devote considerable time and effort trying to be 'good', the Church supported the idea, as did schools and the community at large. So, 'good' and 'bad' were defined and, therefore, there were 'good' and 'bad' people. In reality this concept didn't delve much beneath the surface so, in day-to-day terms, it all came down to behaviour. "You're a bad boy," Mum would say to her disagreeable child, or, "There's a good boy," when he ate his meal.

Of course this was ridiculous. Being naughty or a nuisance is not the same thing as being bad and everyone knew this. So, the words 'good' and 'bad' – however profound to a philosopher or a priest – became devalued, caricatured. Max Miller the comic was a 'bad boy' because he made smutty jokes, everyone's Uncle Reg was 'bad' because he went down the pub for a drink after church on Sunday.

We've moved on, rightly, and are now reluctant to use 'good' and 'bad' quite so casually. Things aren't that simple. Just as we have realised that everyone has male and female qualities in varying degrees, so we accept there is good and bad in all of us. In which case, now that we are dealing in questions of degree, who has the right to punish who?

In terms of the community we have solved the problem neatly by appointing the state to do the dirty work for us, although, interestingly, those delegated with the task of dishing out punishments disguise themselves in wigs and gowns and other paraphernalia, lest they should be mistaken for ordinary people or recognised in the street. And, even though the courts themselves are struggling with just how lenient they should be, this part of the equation more or less still works although for how much longer we shall have to wait and see. Take the problem into schools and people's homes, however, and it is a different picture.

It all depends on whether you believe that punishment is necessary at all. There are those who would have us believe it isn't. The argument goes like this. People who seem anti-social or, for that matter, criminal to the rest of us are merely maladjusted and *it is not their fault.* The important thing is to set a good example, prove to them that behaving in a sensible way and being kind and considerate to others brings greater rewards and they will soon get into line and become kind and considerate themselves. This may take a little time but, with perseverance, this positive approach of rewarding good behaviour rather than punishing bad will produce better and longer lasting results. In other words, there is no need to punish anyone, anytime.

Strange that this type of thinking, popular since the sixties, has coincided with more people being shut away than ever before – so much so that our courts and prisons are bursting at the seams! The question is *can you have reward without punishment?*

Now, I'm not proposing a wholesale return to the days when discipline and violence were synonymous. Not at all. Although, actually, I'm not convinced that physical pain in moderation is not useful in the complex task of bringing up - and educating - a child. By outlawing mild physical punishment we are forcing parents and teachers to rely on more sophisticated psychological ploys which, based on mental rather than physical fear, can be far more damaging in the long term than a slap on the hand. The key is moderation. There is no comparison between a gentle slap from a loving mother and an all-out brutal assault from a drunken father or, for that matter, a malevolent teacher.

We all know that what children really care about is fairness. How many times have you heard a child protest: "But that isn't fair!" A clue! Touchingly, children will put up with almost anything providing it's fair. As you get older you realise that 'fairness' is in pretty short supply, but to kids it's everything. So, to a child, discipline comes into the fairness category. Punish a child and the child will be more concerned with what it's done to deserve it rather than the nature of the punishment itself.

Now, all this depends upon parents being of a reasonable disposition in the first place. In my experience, most are. But not all. Where do parents go wrong? Putting aside pure ignorance and stupidity, which probably only account for a small percentage of parent/child difficulties, the problem is when the parent/child relationship somehow changes from being adult/child, where each has a clearly defined role, into a battle of wills and thus a continuing war to gain the upper hand. No-one likes a control freak and yet this is where both child and parent can so easily end up unless each is aware of the futility of such a battle.

Children discover power very early in life. When they cry they get fed. When they smile, they get a smile back. Little girls find it easy to twist their fathers round their little fingers, boys soon learn how to terrorise their mothers. As with all else, recognising the problem early is the key. Once a pattern of behaviour becomes entrenched, it is much harder (although not impossible) to change. The best scenario is when both parent and child develop an early warning system so that evasive action can be taken swiftly to prevent things getting any worse. This way a mild reprimand, carefully considered, will often do the trick.

I have a friend who has a particularly difficult child where gentle pointers have not been enough. There is something I've noticed, though. The parents don't seem to be able to agree on how to handle the problem, to the extent that they will argue in front of the child as to what the punishment should be. The child – a little boy of five, in this case – has quickly learnt the power of 'divide and rule' and now has huge fun playing off mother against father, a method he will no doubt continue to practice well into his adult life! When and if mother and father get their act together, maybe they will be able to break the deadlock.

Talking about divisions between child and parent it looks to me as though the government has got it seriously wrong (surprise) in this department. Again, misled by the woolly notion of 'rights' – this time it's the children who have them – the state seems hell-bent on driving wedges between children and parents in every conceivable way.

Two examples: how would you feel if your fourteen-year-old daughter had an abortion without you knowing about it? It happens all the time, with the clinical interference of a doctor or some busybody 'out-reach' worker being substituted for the time, compassion and love of a parent. Why? Because the daughter has 'rights'. More likely she is 'scared' to tell her parents. Of course she is! Hasn't this always been so? In a sane society, this sad but not necessarily tragic scenario will be allowed to play itself out within the context of the family. In its manic quest to avoid teenage pregnancies at all costs, by providing the daughter with an alternative, the state will create divisions and a lack of trust within the family that can never be repaired.

Another example. There are periods in a child's life when it has to have total respect for its parents and not question their authority. Now that children have 'rights' of

Views from the Back of a Taxi

which, believe me, they are very much aware, every child who wants to win an argument with, say, an intransigent father, can make up some cock-and-bull story about 'parent abuse' and, before you can say Jack Straw, the social services and police are round. Let me tell you something – *children tell fibs!* Now, there's a revelation. In fact, kids are mostly inveterate liars. We all know that and it doesn't matter because it goes with the territory and they get over it. But you can't seriously base a whole legal process on what a child says.

It goes without saying that there are extreme cases when society does have a duty to protect a child. But what we have now is yet another example of our 'big brother' state knowing best, knowing better, in fact, than parents. It's dangerous, very dangerous.

Still, politics aside, if you want to read a textbook on how to bring up your child, read Dr Spock. If you're the DIY type, my points are simple:

(a) Like any worthwhile relationship in life, successful parent/child teams depend upon mutual respect. Yes, you may know more than your child, but he/she hasn't been spoilt by a lot of rubbish conditioning like you so starts with a clean slate. Always remember you can learn as much from your child as it can from you.

(b) Your child didn't ask to be brought into the world so, whatever goes wrong is *your fault.* That's the responsibility you take on when you have kids. If you don't want it, don't have them. They're not dolls and they're not there for your benefit.

(c) Discipline is an essential part of bringing up a child. Without it a parent is not doing his/her job. If you're lucky,

105

you'll never have to smack your child. Most of us aren't that lucky. If you do, then make sure that the punishment is accompanied by a clear explanation of what the child has done wrong, how you expect things to change and why.

(d) Remember that 'fairness' is the key to the way a child judges a situation. Resist the temptation to use your power as an adult over the child. That includes sarcasm, ridicule, being patronising and inflating your own ego at the child's expense. It might make you feel better but, to the child, at best, you are making a prat of yourself and, at worst, damaging it for life.

(e) Be guided by instinct, love and respect – not by what you read in newspapers or the misguided efforts of politicians and do-gooders trying to teach you how to be a parent. Governments have kept clear of this for centuries - and for good reason. Much cleverer and more knowledgeable politicians and leaders than we have now have chosen wisely to leave the rearing of children to parents.

To state the obvious, but lest we forget, children are our future. When I got married my best man commented that when he had children he hoped he would be proud of them. I replied that if I had children, I hoped they would be proud of me.

I'll leave it to you to decide who was closest to the mark.

The average cost of raising a child to the age of 21 is now £165,668 representing an 18% rise since 2003 - three times the rate of inflation.

The Celebrity Culture

*There's definitely a special relationship between
celebrities and cabbies. Mind you, if we'd
all had to stop to let a famous newsreader
be sick in the gutter at 3am, we might have
a different view of celebrities, too.*

WAS there ever a time when we *didn't* have a celebrity culture?
Well, you might be forgiven for not thinking so, but the fact
is it's always been there. Throughout history we've looked
up to a small group of people, those who performed heroic
deeds, achieved great things or acquired enviable lifestyles.
Still, celebrities aren't what they were.

No-one minds people being famous. It's just that we
used to think they should be famous for a reason, in other
words, it wasn't enough just to be famous for being famous.
Not in today's topsy-turvy world. The distinction between the
real celebrities and the impostors has all but disappeared.

It's not clear whether this new breed of 'celebrities' (the
ones who haven't done anything to deserve fame) is a result
of supply or demand. What came first, the horse or the
cart? The emergence of a group of wannabes who needed
'celebrity' upfront in order to launch their careers on the
back of it – typically 'kiss and tell' bimbos – or the increasing

appetite of the media for stories, any stories, preferably featuring pretty, semi-naked girls?

Pretty girls always make good copy and, for years, the media had to be content with the theatre and show business

to satisfy demand. The trouble was that even the most inventive of publicists found it tough coming up with enough scandal and smut to keep the red-tops happy for long. Let's face it, even an actress cares about her reputation, at least insofar as it affects the parts she gets. So, what seems to have happened is that a completely new breed of celebrities has emerged, only too pleased to base their fame on the very scandals that the tabloids crave. What they do for a living is immaterial.

To be fair, one or two have succeeded in making a career out of such scantily clad celebrity, but it is, frankly, only one or two. And not for long. Without old-fashioned, genuine talent and the hard work to back it up, sustaining fame becomes very tricky indeed.

But we shouldn't worry too much about celebrities; they can and mostly do take care of themselves. Anyway, who in their right mind would want to be one? It might seem like a good idea at the outset, but, like any addiction, once you get hooked, try kicking the habit. You can try, but the habit won't let you go. No, what is more interesting is why *we* need *them*.

We all love heroes. So, let's start there. Young people in particular need older people to inspire them, especially if they demonstrate that with talent, hard work and the right attitude, there are riches waiting at the end of the rainbow. Happily, there are plenty of celebrities out there today who fall into this category. Personal lives aside for the moment, anyone who makes it into the higher ranks of sport or show business deserves our admiration and, if you don't believe me, that's because you have no idea how difficult it is getting there in the first place.

Ask yourself, how many wannabe Wayne Rooneys were clamouring for the job that the one-and-only real Mr Rooney got? The same thing applies to them all. If you've tried, you'll know that these people are different from the rest of us. How did a girl from the Welsh valleys end up as queen of Hollywood? Because not only is Catherine Zeta-Jones beautiful, talented and sexy, she is also ambitious, single-minded, brave, exceedingly smart and hard-working. Michael Douglas realised that and married her. Has it ever occurred to you how astonishing it is that CZ-J is one of less than a handful of truly bankable female movie stars in the world? In the world! And she can't even speak American. Go to Hollywood and you'll see thousands of girls just as gorgeous, just as talented and many of them more so. But Catherine did it. Extraordinary. Don't undervalue that kind of achievement, believe me, it isn't luck and it isn't easy.

So... "If she can do it, so can we!" cries a new generation of lovely young girls. Nonsense, of course, but this is healthy enough and keeps fairyland just within reach. The same with David Beckham, Wayne Rooney, Ant and Dec – all of them, really. These people are cleverer than you think, even if it doesn't always suit them to let you see it.

Now, there's something that's changed. High achievers have to be a bit careful nowadays. Time was when they would be proud to tell you what it took for them to achieve their goals. Nowadays that would not be considered 'cool'. Not only do we want our heroes to achieve great things, we want them to do it easily. Of course, the clever celeb goes along with this. It has to be part of his image. Common sense tells you that David Beckham must work and practise damned hard to be as good a footballer as he is. But have you ever heard him say so? Never. Seeing Beckham bending perfect crosses into the penalty area is only 'cool' if you don't see him practising for hours learning how to do it - while Posh is probably sitting at home with his dinner in the oven. Not part of the image, you see. Not 'cool'.

Ever thought what a destructive word 'cool' is? What does it mean exactly? With it's roots in the American deep south, then adopted by the white urban jazz culture of the fifties and sixties, 'cool' came to mean a kind of effortless style, like the jazz trumpeter who can play an improvised solo off the top of his head, making it up as he goes along, with no music in front of him, no rehearsal, no practise. Apparently. In other words, if you want to be 'cool' the means are as important as the end. Not only do you have to do something well, it has to be made to look easy.

'Cool' is the tennis player who strolls onto court and wins matches without taking his racket out of the bag since his last game, or the businessman who acquires a fat wad, mobile phone and a sharp suit without working long hours or getting stressed, the boy who gets any girl he wants without trying, the girl who is discovered walking down the street and a week later appears on the cover of "Vogue". Get the picture?

'Cool' is success without effort. The problem is it's a myth, and an immensely appealing one to those who want the earth without having to work for it. Which is most of us.

Unfortunately, we've brought up a generation who believe in the myth of 'cool'. Celebrities know this. Not long ago it wasn't cool to come from a middle-class background, so we were subjected to the ridiculous antics of rock stars pretending to be working class, lying about their poor childhoods when, in fact, they came from six-bedroomed houses in Esher and went to private school. Now, we've got to the point where celebrities feel obliged to deny the skill, effort and hard work that lies behind their success. Robbie Williams might make it look as if performing in front of twenty thousand people is a breeze, but he would never tell you the agonies he suffers in the wings. Well, actually, he might - but then is Robbie Williams 'cool'?

What kind of a message does this send out to the young? Exactly the one they want to hear, of course. Along with another myth of our times; the idea that if you want something badly enough you can have it (again, conveniently missing out the 'how') – this has encouraged youngsters to think that if they want to be David Beckham all they have to do is kick a ball around and, magically, someone will come along, discover them and sign them up for MU or Real Madrid.

What does our new breed of 'famous for being famous' represent? Exactly this idea. That you can be famous without doing anything to deserve it; all you need is the desire, the opportunity and Max Clifford will do the rest. How cool is that? How sad, too.

*Paris Hilton commands £500,000 to show
up at a party. "All I have to do is wave like
this", she says imitating the Queen.*

The Press

Have you thought how often you hear an important news
item from a taxi driver before you've read it or seem
it on television? Media people spend loads of time in
the back of cabs, time that can be highly productive
- depending on who was there before them.

LET'S all go shoot the messenger! That is if you don't like
the news, and most of us don't most of the time.

Sorry to disillusion you but the problems we face *are not*
the media's fault.

The trouble is we don't always like what we read, so
we would rather not believe it – therefore, the media must
be wrong. We go into denial and the media take the stick.
Actually, the reverse is the case. Hardly anything you read
or hear in the media is untrue. It may not necessarily be
expressed in language you appreciate, it may not always
re-enforce your own views but, ninety-nine times out of a
hundred, it is accurate. Why? Because otherwise newspapers,
magazines and the broadcasters would be in court all the
time. And they're not.

It must be obvious that for most of the time the present
government has been in power, the media, particularly the
press, have been the only effective opposition we've had. If Her
Majesty's Opposition can really get its act together this might

be different but, as things stand, and with the BBC reduced to re-hashing press releases from 10 Downing Street (or, occasionally Buckingham Palace), newspapers have become the only remaining independent voice of the people. So, whether you like them or not, the alternative is a lot worse.

What would the alternative be? Start with the fact that when he first goes to Westminster every politician believes he is right. Politics isn't quite a religion but very nearly. Remember that not so long ago (we're talking Gunpowder Plot) people were being killed in their thousands in this country because they practised a slightly different version of Christianity than the 'ruling party'. Make no mistake, those doing the killing weren't madmen - quite the reverse, they were the cleverest, best-educated people of their time. But, sadly, they were consumed with a passion (or had convinced themselves) that Catholics were so bad they should be exterminated. And because they were in power they could do it. And they did. Why? Because they believed they were right.

Yes, politicians believe they are right so, when they get criticised, not only don't they like it, they get frustrated. To start with, they'll argue their points believing that anyone silly enough to disagree with them can be quickly persuaded to see the obvious error of their ways. It's when this doesn't happen, when, to their utter amazement, others put forward contrary, well-reasoned arguments that the trouble starts. The temptation to use their power to smother the opposition becomes irresistible. The end begins to justify the means.

This is what we have seen increasingly during the last ten years. The media have frequently opposed those zealously intent upon reform at all costs and so, rather than take the time to debate and discuss the issues, the government has set out to manipulate and control the media. To stifle the criticism. The spectacle of the BBC caving in so quickly following the Andrew

Gilligan debacle and two sham 'enquiries', was seriously depressing. Half a century of carefully nurtured independence of mind and spirit blown away in a couple of weeks.

The fact that this hasn't happened to newspapers, which are still self-regulated and, by and large, responsible, is a minor miracle. Therefore, at this moment in time the newspapers are free to say what they think within the limits of the law as it stands. The trouble is politicians have the power to change the law. Of course, even they won't attempt to introduce legislation preventing newspapers from criticising them – they know they'd never get it through. Instead, they will start by pecking around the perimeter, probably starting with new laws on privacy.

This is clever, touching as it does a raw nerve amongst the British who have always cherished the notion that we should all be allowed a 'private' life safe from the prying eyes of others (a peculiarly Victorian notion which doesn't stand too close an examination, but that's for another day). Anyway, the only time the press delve into people's private lives is when there is something of much greater consequence at stake - for example, a public figure whose judgement in his private life is so disastrous that it becomes arguable whether he is fit for public office at all. But could you put your hand on your heart and say that, for the likes of you and I, the intrusion of the media into our private lives is an issue? Why should they be interested in us? Do you actually *know* anyone personally who has suffered as a result of the press delving into their personal lives? I doubt it.

In France, of course, politicians and public figures enjoy the protection of the law when it comes to their private lives. This is why they can have presidents and prime ministers who can keep permanent mistresses at all times, not to mention illegitimate children and dubious business 'interests'. I can see our government latching on to this before long on the basis that we're all in the EU and it isn't fair to have one set of regulations in France and another in the UK. Thus, Tessa Jowell's husband, at the time of writing on trial in Italy on charges of tax evasion (amongst other things), would never have been exposed.

Make no mistake about it, the introduction of new privacy laws will be the beginning of a process designed to curb the freedom of the press. Once the process has started, there will be no stopping it. While the Government says on the one hand that it wishes to protect privacy, the outcome will be exactly the opposite. An exact parallel, in fact, to the new anti-terrorist laws – brought in under the guise of protecting our freedom but in reality providing the government with exactly the powers they want to limit it.

Freedom of the press is one of the few things we have left of the old order where free speech, the right to challenge the mighty and the righteous, was enshrined in our unwritten constitution and protected by the law of the land. All of this is now under threat and we are in real danger of going backwards. Life is becoming ruder and cruder as the intricate checks and balances we have inherited are swept away with little of consequence being put in their place.

Freedom of speech and freedom of the press are inexorably intertwined. Whatever its excesses and absurdities, however laughable it may sometimes appear to be, we must preserve the freedom of the press at all costs. For the foreseeable future it may be the only defence we have against the relentless attempts to control our opinions, our views and our lives by those we have no good reason trust.

With democracy on its knees we need all the help we can get in working out who's with us and who's against us.

You don't protect our liberties by withdrawing them.

Television

It's not surprising that people are bewildered by what is happening to our television industry and taxi drivers are no exception. They tend to watch the box quite a bit, not always at peak time, and want some straight answers. So, here goes...

DOES anyone watch television anymore? The answer must be 'yes', but one wonders sometimes.

I don't know about you but I get an awful lot of people saying they 'can't be bothered' or 'there's nothing worth watching anymore'. Most people I talk to don't like the so-called reality shows, are fed up with the soaps and don't believe the news. More and more men seem to be watching sport on Sky. Response to drama is patchy and everyone says that humour in the shape of sitcoms and light entertainment is all but extinct. Who is it that likes 'alternative' comedy? I haven't met a single soul, have you?

It's not long ago when television was the most powerful force in our lives - when the Prime Minister could go on BBC knowing that the majority of the population would be watching. Today, he'd be better off writing a piece in 'The Sun'. Now, TV takes its place amongst the myriad of distractions available to us in our leisure hours and, even then, doesn't always fare too well. It's lost its place in our minds and hearts. Why?

In the beginning television was a glorious monopoly. Launched soon after the war and entrusted to the nation's broadcaster, the BBC, TV started well enough guided by the principles of its founder, Lord John Reith. It may seem paternalistic in hindsight, but Reith's idea that a national broadcasting service had a responsibility to educate as well as entertain, should offer a wide range of subject matter and pursue a policy of balanced programming had a great deal of merit. Prior to television radio had been seen as a huge success following these principles and there seemed little reason to re-invent the wheel.

When the BBC's monopoly was broken by the introduction of a second channel, ITV, despite much consternation at the time, it was entirely staffed by BBC-trained personnel who, whilst they may have liked to perceive themselves as sharper and more commercial, ran ITV in pretty much the same way as they'd run the Beeb. Not long afterwards both BBC and ITV were rewarded by getting second channels, BBC2 and Channel 4, and so the ship sailed happily on. A population of 55 million people serviced by four TV channels, two 'popular' and two 'specialist'. Pretty soon it happened that the total advertising revenue of ITV more or less equated with the license fees funding the BBC and, apart from the ad breaks on the commercial channels, there was little to choose between them.

It's also worth dwelling for a moment on how cleverly ITV had been structured at the outset. A system of franchises dividing the country up into regions meant that each company had to provide a full local service in their area as well as feeding in to the national network. The effect of this was to create centres of excellence throughout the country competing with each for the 'prize' of producing programmes worthy of network transmission. No pipe dream this as the emergence of Granada in Manchester, Yorkshire in Leeds and Tyne Tees as centres of broadcasting excellence quickly proved - all of them giving the London and southern franchisees a run for their money. With the BBC carrying on broadly in its Reithian tradition, we were making the finest programmes in the world and British TV enjoyed its golden years.

What happened? Of course, control of the airwaves has, ironically, always been seen as imperative for governments. I say 'ironically' because what could be more abstract than an airwave? Nevertheless, with all broadcasting frequencies licensed by the government – and the BBC funded effectively by a tax – it is the government who ultimately controls broadcasting. Witness the paranoia over pirate radio in the 60's and 70's. Harmless DJ's broadcasting from ships outside British waters who, technically, avoided the necessity to pay for their frequencies. You'd have thought they were warships, judging by the way the government couldn't wipe them out quickly enough! Make no mistake, broadcasting, including ITV, has always been a heavily regulated industry.

You'll remember that in the later years of the Thatcher government there was a war on monopolies. Taking a leaf out of her American friends' book, Mrs T became obsessed with the notion of consumerism and the idea that competition in the marketplace always benefits the consumer. Why only four TV stations? Let's see how many the 'market' will stand. So, along came Channel 5, a station which never had a remit, never established a market for itself and still hasn't. Then came satellite. Then digital. With the advent of Sky, families who used to receive only four or five channels on their TV sets suddenly had the opportunity to watch fifty or sixty, providing they could afford the subscription.

Here is where the tragedy of television in the last fifteen years lies; the fact that the BBC and ITV, the terrestrial broadcasters as they are now called, caved in so quickly and easily to competition from another form of television broadcasting which actually charged for its service. Who would have thought that after nearly half a century of supplying a service *for nothing* (because that's how it seems to the recipient) the established broadcasters simply could not react quickly and effectively enough to ward off a predator with no ambitions (nor means) to match them in terms of programme quality or content, and who was proposing to charge hundreds of pounds a year for the privilege of being received? In fact, so accommodating were ITV and BBC that they actually sold their programming to Sky! The last time a British industry did that was when the old British Motor Corporation sent envoys to Japan to teach them how to build cars. Look what happened after that.

You see, none of these other channels will ever be able to make for themselves the kind of stuff that ITV and the BBC have been producing for years. With costs of drama, for example, running at over ¾ million pounds an hour, they will never have enough viewers or a large enough audience to command sufficient revenue. The problem is that they will deprive the BBC and ITV of enough viewers to prevent them doing it either. All those glorious period dramas will become a thing of the past. In fact, anything remotely expensive, which includes big music shows, lavish light entertainment, even those wonderful nature shows, will eventually disappear or, at least, become infrequent on our screens. Needless to say, it will take longer for the BBC to decline – for the time being it has the edge over its commercial competitor – because there will be a protracted process of political argument about its license fee or even, in the future, subsidy. But the end result, governed by Mrs Thatcher's and, subsequently, Tony Blair's, much-loved market forces will be the same.

And where does digital fit into all this? In my view it's a complete red herring. Who cares how the signal is transmitted if the programme is rubbish? A marginally better quality of picture or sound is a high price to pay if the programme being delivered isn't worth watching. Yet the government, in partnership with the broadcasters, has invested billions in digital. Why? Presumably, because it's easier to invest in technology than creativity. You know where you stand with technology, creativity is rather harder to manage. Most of it, incidentally, has disappeared down the same black hole as the funding for the Millennium Dome. Anyway, no amount of investment in hardware will make up for poor quality software, in this case television programmes. That's where the problem lies and there's not much sign of it getting better.

It may occur to you that a multi-channel system works perfectly well in the States, so why not here? Something that may have spurred Mrs Thatcher on when she started all this. The answer, of course, is that the American audience is *five times* the size of ours. Unfortunately, the programmes cost us the same to make. What about the largely expanded United States of Europe, I hear you cry? Possibly, if the day comes when we all speak the same language and share the same culture, then there may be such a thing as true Pan-European programme making. But that, my friends, is a hundred years away and, for now, we can't bear to watch each other's programmes.

In the meantime if you want evidence that what I'm saying is true, just look at your current TV listings. Isn't it obvious that the broadcasters are stretching their programme budgets to the limit? ITV's terrestrial audience has fallen in real terms by more than 40% in the last ten years, although they'll tell you something different. The BBC, too, has seen its audience share dropping just as fast, amidst increasing opposition to the level of the license fee or even whether it is justified at all.

The result? Standards will continue to fall. The reality shows, admittedly capable of pulling in largish audiences in the short term, are there not just because they are popular with the audience but because they are cheap. Daytime programming almost entirely features members of the public, doing for free what professionals once got paid for. And it will get worse.

The real puzzle is how on earth the BBC and ITV allowed this unconditional surrender to happen in the first place. You'd have thought they would have seen off Rupert Murdoch with their eyes shut. As always it comes down to people. Remember Lew Grade allegedly saying that owning a TV station was a license to print money? Broadcasting in this country had things its own way for such a long period of time it bred a generation of 'fair-weather' managers who were only capable of running an inherently profitable business. When things got tough, suddenly but not unpredictably, they weren't up to it. First they shut their eyes, buried their head in the sand, then panicked and did what all accountants do - started to cut costs. Not good enough gals and guys and we're all the losers.

And I can't see it getting any better.

Recent research has shown that young children prefer to look at a blank TV screen than at the face of another human being

The Meaning of Life

An evergreen if ever there was one! No problem,
though, given a regulation thirty-minute ride from
South Kensington to Fenchurch Street, especially if
you get stuck in roadworks on the Embankment.

I LIKE the story about the guy who gets into his car one
summer's morning to discover a ladybird on the dashboard.
But that's probably because I made it up. Anyway, reluctant
to disturb the insect, he drives thirty miles to a series of
meetings, returning home later in the day, still with the
ladybird for company. Arriving at his house he gets out of the
car. As he does so, the ladybird takes wing and flies away.

The point of the story is that the ladybird knows
absolutely nothing about what has happened. In our world
the little fella has been on a journey, it has travelled past
buildings, streams, countryside, animals in fields, crossed
level crossings, stopped at crossroads, witnessed the rising and
setting of the sun, the changes in the weather, heard music
on the radio – a thousand things. But, in the insect world,
the ladybird has merely lost a little time in between flying off
a leaf and returning to it.

Of course, the ladybird possesses intelligence, enough, in
fact, to survive successfully in a hostile world, reproduce and
ensure the survival of its species. No mean feat, you might

say. And yet this same intelligence is far from sufficient to understand the journey it has experienced.

If we can accept the likelihood that we rank fairly lowly in the inter-galactic intelligence league, then it is possible to see how we, too, may be part of someone else's journey, which we cannot begin to comprehend.

This is something the church has been telling us down the centuries, but few of us have grasped. Although that is not to say the idea is necessarily religious.

The point is this: if we *are* part of someone else's grand scheme, there may be no meaning in our lives, not as far as we are concerned anyway, although we might be fulfilling some small purpose in the scheme of a greater being. After all, charming though the ladybird is, it would be overstating the case to say it is important to us.

However, we have become so accustomed to understanding everything that it is hard for us to get our heads around our insignificance on a truly universal (in the true sense of the word) scale. The first chapter of "The Hitch Hikers Guide to the Galaxy" depicts a huge inter-galactic battle, which, in the end, didn't count for very much because it all happened in a space not much larger than the end of a pin. Make no mistake, that *is* us.

In the meantime, we seek and want purpose in our lives. To me it has always been enough to try to do the best I can for myself, my family and my immediate community of friends, colleagues and acquaintances. This is pretty hard to do well, but if everyone achieved this modest objective, it would, quite literally, change the world.

But I know this does not seem enough for some, those with a drive and an ambition to make a wider, more public contribution to the good of mankind. Admirable though this may be, such people would be well advised not to get too distracted by "the meaning of life". For all the difference it will make day-to-day, it's not worth dwelling on. Instead, they should leave the bigger questions to philosophers and poets and concentrate on living their lives guided by a set of well-tried and tested principles. The Ten Commandments is a pretty good place to start. By all means try to leave the world a better place than you found it, but don't get lost in delusions of self-importance and the false belief that ends justify means – they don't and yet it's the commonest mistake leaders make. We are seeing it all around us now. History proves the point over and over again.

Instead, settle for the notion that "the meaning of life" is merely the name you give to your own life. And then set about working that out for yourself. Believe me, it's a lot more practical.

13 people have been born in the world in the time it takes you to read this sentence

Management

Last year more than £50b of British assets were snapped up by foreign firms. Would you put your faith in our managers anymore? Are they managing in the real sense of the word, or merely presiding over the sale of the family silver?

NOWADAYS, people seem to prefer relationships with computers than with other human beings.

Putting aside for a moment the increasingly large number of people working from home, even those who still go to the office sit in front of their desktops all day long with little or no interface with those around them. Half the time it is impossible to know what they're doing and if you try to look over their shoulders, they press a key to make sure you won't find out! Worse, people at adjacent desks are more likely to e-mail each other than get up to have a conversation.

How can you manage people when everyone is doing everything by e-mail?

I'm not going to bang on about the computer being the curse of our age. It's far too useful and has opened up too many genuinely fresh opportunities to say that. But I am convinced that in many areas of life, the workplace being one, it has created a form of dependence, which, conveniently exploited, can be used to let us all off the hook. Naturally we look for ways to get shot of responsibility and the computer is the answer. Why say "human error" when you can cite "computer error" instead. It's something to hide behind. Today, when an aircraft crashes killing hundreds of people it's blamed on the computer, not the pilot.

What worries me more though is, firstly, the effect of computers on people's social lives and, secondly, what they are doing to business. Particularly, the latter. Those with any sense will always stay in touch with other people, make the effort to tear themselves away from their friendly, reassuring laptop and indulge in man's oldest leisure pursuit – namely, seeking out the company of others. What is harder to fathom is the effect on what we used to call "Management and Motivation".

Reduced to the most basic level, business is about selling. If you don't sell, you ain't got no customers and, without customers, you don't have a business. Tell me a business which works any other way? You won't be able to think of one. Needless to say, the more competition you have or the less appealing your product, the harder you'll have to sell. And, as any good businessman knows, for optimum results, the 'selling' ethos has to run right the way through an organisation. You can't simply employ a sales force so that no-one else has to worry about turnover.

Even though a large number of staff, even most of them, may not be directly engaged in selling on an hour-to-hour, day-to-day basis, they all need to feel part of the process, to believe that what they are doing is worthwhile and successful. After all, wages and bonuses aside, it's what makes work enjoyable and fulfilling – that is, if you're lucky enough to have good managers who understand this and know how to make it work.

Successful companies have always taken the time and trouble to make sure that staff at all levels are 'engaged' in helping the business do well and feel part of it. But this is a 'hands-on', person-to-person process, requiring people to work alongside each other, to be in the same place at the same time and to exchange ideas and experiences. Then you can start 'managing' them. The problem arises when this situation no longer occurs. That's what is worrying about the computer based work ethic and people working from home. If all jobs were simply task orientated it wouldn't matter but, if you want ideas, creativity and teamwork, people have to work together, talk together and *think* together. That's when two plus two might just add up to five.

Somewhere in all this is another factor, namely, that the term 'management' is increasingly felt to be offensive. People don't want to be managed anymore, it's as if it infringes their human rights. I'm not sure they want to learn either, to broaden their skill base and move ahead as individuals. True, the relationship between 'boss' and 'employee' can be tricky. In fact, there is a strong moral argument that says such a relationship is flawed, based as it is on the premise of two people exploiting one another – the boss demanding more for less, the employee striving to achieve the opposite. And, whilst it is still widely assumed that the boss has the upper hand, in reality, this is seldom the case. Employment legislation has put paid to that. Nevertheless, it is still the best arrangement we've come up. In fact, I'm astonished by the number of people who seem to really enjoy their jobs, despite the trials and tribulations of being 'employed'.

Oh, and before anyone shouts 'self-employment', let me say this. Yes, I know lots of self-employed people and, taking as read the character and survival instinct you need to work for yourself, I do believe that in the longer term they have a better time of it than people who are employed. I also happen to think they are more secure. But self-employment is still for the few and, anyway, we can't leave the future of our economy to the self-employed. Sadly, it is not often that a Richard Branson or an Alan Sugar emerges from the ranks to grow a business of any scale or significance. In the meantime, we need the huge conglomerates and multi-nationals to drive the economy, especially on the world stage.

It is these large companies that need better managers than ever before and I'm not sure they're getting them. I don't see how they can be. Three things have dogged British industry for the last fifty years (a) lack of institutional investment in the future of industry, especially manufacturing (b) short-term thinking by senior management and (c) the reluctance of the workforce to strive whole-heartedly for the success of the companies they work for.

Now, of course, these problems are inter-dependent. How can you expect workforces to take a long term view and increase productivity when they see their bosses failing to secure the investment the business obviously requires, not to mention lining their own pockets in the short term? How can banks and lending institutions be expected to invest when they see senior management adopting a series of short-term 'get-rich-quick' tactics? And how can senior management feel their futures are secure when they are briefed to prop up share prices rather than plan and grow the business in the long term? Talk about a vicious circle.

The answer to all this is confidence. And this is what we have lost to a large degree. It's also why we've sold off so much of the family silver. Short-termism has been rife in the UK for a long time now. And if anyone thinks that in the new 'global' society it doesn't matter who owns companies, think again. The wealth a company creates goes back to the place where it is owned. If this isn't clear, think of the UK as a region within the global structure – do you want to live in a poor region or a rich one?

Look at America. If 'global' worked then every state, every big city would be as affluent as the next, all sharing equally in the wealth generated by the whole. Not so. Sorry. It's vital that we keep ownership of our large companies and enterprises. Don't be fooled by the 'global' argument, it's an excuse for the self-serving actions of greedy shareholders. The truth is that when one of these businesses gets sold to the French, the Germans or the Japanese, a relatively small number of individual shareholders and institutions (usually including the top slice of management) enjoy gigantic financial windfalls. Of course, it's a one-off event. Once those businesses have gone they are gone forever and with them goes the wealth they created and the contribution they made to our standard of living. We want our people to be employed *and* retain the fruits of their labours. Keeping people in jobs may make a Labour government's statistics look good, but it's a poor substitute to having them create wealth for the country.

Here's another question. Why is it that an overseas buyer can manage a British company better than we can? On the basis that all else is equal, which it usually is, the only plausible reason is that they have better managers. Sad, isn't it?

Management is about people and (some would say unfortunately) you can't manage people by bossing them around and issuing orders you expect them to obey. It's been a long time since you could run a business like the army. Apart from anything else, increasingly burdensome employment legislation won't let you. Management by example, skill, persuasion and motivation, coupled with experience is the only way to do it and that's difficult to teach. This means we need really good managers who have talent, training and, hopefully, an understanding of human nature. You don't come across many of those, do you?

The youth culture doesn't help. I watched a documentary about an American company in which representatives of every level of management were featured. The interesting thing was how those levels were reflected in the ages of the people concerned. Junior managers were in their thirties, middle managers in their forties and senior managers in their fifties. The chairmen and CEO were in their sixties! It occurred to me that this is not at all what we have in the UK. You could reduce all those age groups by ten to fifteen years. Let's face it, we must be one of the few if not the only country in the world where it would be possible to elect a Prime Minister in his early forties, a man who, by definition, will be learning on the job – and, potentially, making hugely expensive mistakes in the process.

There is a time in life for everything. If you want a really good senior manager you want someone who is no longer distracted by the task of bringing up a young family, paying a mortgage, worrying about his own finances and prospects. He doesn't necessarily need the energy, single-mindedness or aggression of a younger man – what he does need is experience of life, a little humility and real knowledge of the job at hand. In short, he needs to have been round the block a few times. You don't get these qualities in people in their thirties.

Instead of recognising this, we promote youngsters into jobs they are not fit to take on and throw older, wiser people on the scrapheap. Why? To my knowledge no-one else in the world does this.

Do you understand that? I don't.

There are only 15 women in top executive positions in FTSE 100 companies compared to 376 men.

Lookism

You'll see lots of good looking, fashionably dressed people hailing taxis in every major city in the UK. Looks and success appear to go together. But do they - or is this just another twenty-first century fad? A very witty driver I met coined the word 'lookism' to describe this kind of discrimination.

HE may have invented the word, I'm not sure. What it means is that we live in a society that discriminates against people because of how they look. And, boy, if that's true, what a price we pay for it!

There can be no question that in today's world appearances are everything, or very nearly. The word 'image', now accepted as part of the normal currency of professional, commercial and public life, is a purely visual reference and has it's roots in how people, things and situations 'look' rather than how they 'are'. And, increasingly, advancing technology means that we are exposed to more images, more often than ever before.

So, why have we become so content to judge everything, people included, on the basis of appearances? Plus the fact that whereas 'beauty used to be in the eye of the beholder', now we have a consensus of what is beautiful and what isn't. What's worse, we now make important decisions based on looks. For example, it is almost impossible nowadays to imagine electing a leader of a political party or a Prime Minister who wasn't 'good looking'. Why, for God's sake?

Part of the reason could be that we no longer live in a society where good looks are considered a 'gift'. Rather, we've come to regard beauty as something to which all of us can and should aspire, even if we weren't blessed with it at birth. It's a matter of effort and hard work. Therefore, if someone is plain, we conclude they're lazy or can't be bothered to look better. As a result, that person loses our respect and admiration. By contrast, good-looking people are praiseworthy because they have obviously 'succeeded' in making the most of their appearance.

Go back a little in history and you will see that this wasn't always so. Before the days of cameras, television and film – not to mention fashion-for-all, exercise videos and plastic surgery - what people looked like was not widely known. In those days you couldn't judge people on their appearance because you had no way of knowing what they looked like! Unless you'd actually met someone, you were reliant upon paintings and prints, nearly always concocted by artists in the pay of the subject and charged with the job of presenting the most flattering likeness possible. And judging by the artists' best results, some of them must have been pretty hideous!

The fact remains that, deprived of the tools of mass visual communication, the public had little choice but to judge others on the basis of what they said and did unless, of course, they were privileged to have met and talked face-to-face – still, in my opinion, the only real way to form a sound judgement of another human being.

Today, all this has been circumvented. We are subjected to a relentless stream of images, many of them manipulated, so it's not surprising that we make judgements about people according to what we see of them rather than what we know about them. The unfortunate thing is that this habit of judging by appearances has spilt over into every aspect of our lives.

I'll give you an example. I know a young woman who is a teacher – and a very good one. Although attractive and outgoing, she was, until recently, considerably overweight. In the last year she has lost the best part of five stone and now looks gorgeous, without any exaggeration, like a model. She says it has changed her life. Not only does everyone want to meet and talk to her wherever she goes, even the children she teaches regard her with increased respect and admiration. Now, of course, getting herself fit and trim, with everything that involves – self-discipline, determination, diet, exercise and so on - is something to be admired. But, has it made her a better teacher? No, it hasn't. Has it made her a better role model for those kids? According to our current culture, yes, it has. She has achieved what many of those children will want to achieve themselves, to be beautiful. But, is this the way we want our kids to think?

Unfortunately, this leads to more sinister consequences. It is often remarked on how girls have taken up smoking more than ever before, many of them at a very young age. Drive past your local school at the end of the day and you will see dozens of stick thin young girls lighting up while they wait for their mums to pick them up. Ask a fourteen year old why she smokes and she'll give you all kinds of reasons other than the truth – which is: smoking cigarettes stops you getting fat. Or, that's what they think. Sadly, this is reinforced when they see stick-thin female celebrities smoking or, for that matter, snorting coke.

I hate to think how many impressionable young girls must be thinking what a good idea it is to get onto cocaine as quickly as possible so that they will end up looking (and earning) like Kate Moss. Those endless images of her in the papers linked to headlines about drug-taking have done no good at all. Young people can't always distinguish between cause and effect – to you or I Kate Moss may seem incredibly lucky not to have become a raddled old cow like many of her addicted contemporaries, to the young it's a short shift of logic to believe that she looks the way she does *because* she snorts coke.

It's true that beauty is hypnotic. We will always be lured into treating beautiful people more generously, forgiving them more readily, helping and encouraging them more frequently, falling in love with them more easily. But, surely, we should be getting better at dealing with all this, not worse!

It's nice if the captain of the 747 flying you across the Atlantic is in his late forties, tanned and good-looking with greying sideburns, but, given the choice, would you exchange him for an ugly guy who was a better pilot? Difficult one. The trouble is that for some reason good looks are re-assuring. We *assume* that the better-looking man is the better pilot, until proved otherwise. Trouble is by then it might be too late. Take another scenario. Suppose the ugly guy was given the chance to show you he was better qualified for the job, he'd be the one who'd have to prove himself, wouldn't he? The onus would be on him, not the other way around.

Puzzling. But there's another factor that may explain the phenomenon quite simply. Namely, judging people and things by appearances is easy. It's instant and doesn't require the brain to be engaged. That's very appealing. We live in a world of snap decisions, quick fixes and instant judgements. Assessing someone on their looks is a lazy, slapdash, irresponsible thing to do. Maybe that's why it's so popular.

We need to get back to taking a more rounded view of our leaders, colleagues and counterparts. Only then will we be able to put our hands on our hearts knowing that we are providing people with equal opportunities regardless of race, colour, creed, age - *and looks.*

"Kate Moss woke up looking like she had just stepped off a catwalk, while I had dribble all over my chin."

BIG BROTHER'S JANE GOODY ON MEETING THE
SUPERMODEL ON A FLIGHT TO NEW YORK

Health

*This could be the taxi driver's Achilles heel. How can a
sedentary job, with high stress levels and unsociable hours
have anything to commend it in the health stakes? Good
job for the brain, you might say, but not the body.*

"AS long as you have your health", the saying goes. Not
entirely true, of course - I know people who are perfectly well
but still manage to make a complete mess of things – but, I'd
have to agree, you won't get much fun out of life if you're ill.

The problem comes when we think we can 'delegate' our
health to others. We're so used to the idea that 'experts' will
take care of us when things go wrong, that we've given up on
the idea of looking after ourselves.

Some of my male friends know more about their cars
than their own bodies, not to mention their minds.

It is extraordinary we understand so little about what's
going on under our skin. Sure, I was taught the elementary
facts about the organs and what they do, more often by
dissecting very small creatures in the school labs than by
studying the human body itself, but the whole business
seemed surreal as if it had very little to do with me.

A couple of years ago I went to an exhibition of 'plasticized'
bodies put on by a rather scary German gentleman which,
at the time, was travelling the rounds. Not surprisingly it

was well publicised, mostly attracting derisive and shocked reactions from the media who seemed to have real ethical problems (not something the media is noted for) with the idea of preserving real human bodies and exhibiting them. The general conclusion was that the whole thing was salacious and in poor taste. I went out of curiosity and bravado.

It was a revelation.

Here, for the first time, were bodies, organs, which I could associate with my own. Not only that, it was beautiful. I don't quite know how but the scary German had actually managed to make dissected human remains look like pieces of sculpture. Extraordinary. I came away having learnt more about myself in an afternoon than in all those biology lessons put together.

Now, I'm no expert, but I've learnt enough about the medical profession to realise that the extent of their expertise is greatly exaggerated due to the pitiful ignorance of their patients - with a large dose of myth and mysticism thrown in.

I watched a television programme the other day which, albeit reluctantly, concluded that in all probability the ancient art of acupuncture actually worked and that 'conventional' medicine would do well to embrace it and other 'alternative' forms of medicine, too.

Tell me something. When these 'alternative' treatments have been around for thousands of years, why do doctors refer to their own drug-orientated methods as 'conventional'? It should be the other way round! We've only had modern medicine for the last hundred and fifty years since Pasteur discovered germ theory. In fact, it wasn't until 1929 that Alexander Fleming came up with penicillin, the first modern drug and still, surprisingly, the most widely used. That was the beginning of the pharmacological industry and the idea that if you wanted to cure anything caused by bacteria you could just take a drug. They still can't cure hundreds of conditions caused by viruses, not to mention a whole host of diseases to do with the immune system such as MS and Motor Neurone disease. As a matter of fact, they can't cure the common cold.

How can these people pronounce judgement on other treatments, which have proven themselves over thousands of years? How can they justify their 'scientific' approach which, in reality, doesn't demand any understanding of how or why their drugs work, only that 'research' and 'testing' is carried out on a wide enough scale to 'prove' that they do. That's not science, it's market research!

Now, if you think I'm being uncharitable to modern medicine let me put that straight. I'm not against the occasional aspirin or anti-biotic. What I don't like is our unquestioning reliance on drugs, taken in large quantities over long periods of time. Plus, I'm a great fan of surgeons. Surgery is not the same thing as pharmacology. At the most basic level the body is a machine and may require re-building, adjusting and mending from time to time. Like herbalism, homeopathy, acupuncture, faith healing (to name but a few ancient medical treatments), surgery goes back thousands of years, too, and has come on in leaps and bounds. Very little to do with science, of course, more to do with craftsmanship and skill, qualities I admire and can relate to. No, it's the drugs that worry me.

Putting aside for a moment the political power of pharmaceutical companies, we should be concerned about the routine prescribing of 'medical' drugs and the 'spin-off' effect on drug taking generally which is now reaching crisis point in most developed countries. Yes, it's convenient to make a distinction between the two, but the fact remains that morphine (widely used for pain control in hospitals) is the same thing as heroin, which is illegal when used to treat 'pain' on the street. I can't quite square this. Dependence is dependence, addiction is addiction and drugs are drugs.

We need to look at the long-term effects on the human body of taking powerful drugs to relieve symptoms when there are other far less harmful alternatives available. It is perfectly possible, for example, to perform open-heart surgery using acupuncture instead of anaesthetic. The patient is conscious throughout the operation and is out of bed two days later with no side effects. What's more, the cost of the whole procedure is halved. This is done routinely in China and demonstrates perfectly how the ancient arts of surgery and, in this case, acupuncture can work hand in hand.

Here's another thing. You must have heard the experts argue that the reason alternative treatments work is because of the 'placebo' effect. For example, it's not the homeopathic pills that cure you, it's the 'idea' that you will get better because you're taking them. The 'placebo' effect is well-known and, indeed, is routinely taken into account when drug companies conduct their 'research'. Those patients who took the 'placebo', the dummy tablet, and improved anyway are discarded from the analysis of results. Don't you think it's interesting that these patients get better? Isn't that important in itself?

What is going on, of course, is that this kind of research throws up time and time again that the placebo effect is significant, in other words some patients get better *if they only believe they are being treated.* Well, it may suit the drug companies to ignore this, but I think it deserves more detailed attention. It won't, of course, because drug companies can't earn money out of licensing dummy pills. No side effects, though.

I'm also desperately worried about vaccination. Regardless of the 'scientific' case to the contrary, I can't imagine what we are doing to little babies pumping them full of chemicals to *prevent* them getting ill. What I do know is that this has become a huge worldwide industry, fuelled by the financial ambitions of the pharmaceutical companies and governments who seek ever-increasing control over our daily lives. That's not to say immunisation might not have a place in the greater scheme of things – particularly in those rare instances nowadays when there is a real risk of widespread infection, most obviously in the under-developed countries – but, as a blanket measure here, I don't think so. To argue that by immunising small babies against flu the NHS will save large sums of money later, is both specious and lamentable. Let's at least wait until people get ill before we start shoving potentially harmful drugs down their throats or, in this case, injecting them into their upper arms and bottoms.

Besides which, yet again, we come up against the element of compulsion. I have no doubt that the government would love to enforce stronger legislation so that parents who refuse to co-operate with the Chief Medical Officer's latest whim to introduce yet another vaccine (I think the current total is five) can be suitably punished. Power to the parents, I say. Given the chance, and free from external interference, young humans will develop their own highly effective immune systems and, in these days of relatively good nutrition and hygiene, we should not be over concerned about frequent and untreatable epidemics.

Of course, the Chief Medical Officer would say that the very fact we don't have plagues and diphtheria on the scale we used to is a tribute to the success of vaccination programmes over the last fifty years. I don't believe that, there are simply too many other factors involved. Either way, if vaccination once had a role to play, it's worked its way out of a job now.

When it comes down to it, your health is your business. Today, with the Internet, we have the best chance ever to learn about ourselves and what makes us tick. Modern medicine, despite it's arrogance, is still too young and too unproven to claim this territory as it's own. Its practitioners may claim to be 'scientists' but, in reality, they're not and, anyway, so what? Like so much other science, medical research, by which I mean pharmaceutical testing, has its routes in trial and error rather than an in-depth understanding of what is going on in the human body. Too many drugs to mention, from Penicillin to Viagra, have been discovered by accident to give us real confidence in medical 'science'.

It's not that I'm ungrateful, but a little less faith in what we have now and rather more respect for treatments that have evolved over thousands of years, would not go amiss.

As always, be suspicious rather than afraid of Big Brother and set about learning as much as you can about yourself. Learn. Take responsibility.

You won't regret it.

PS - Here's a tip, eat slowly! The fact that for hundreds of years meals have been social occasions with food prepared and served course by course, interspersed with conversation and good cheer is no coincidence. It slows you down and gives the digestive system a chance to do its job properly. Even in these frenetic times people generally don't choose to eat alone. The 'British Rail' hamburger, consumed on the 5.58 to Sidcup, washed down with a bottle of Mexican beer whilst speaking to home on the mobile, is a road to ruin. It's also the best way I know to put on weight. Take your time, sit down to eat with family and friends, chew your food and get your life back.

Government statistics reveal that nearly twenty people a week die as a result of taking prescription drugs. Last year, for the first time ever, the figure exceeded 1,000 cases.

Happiness

Everyone from Miss World to Gordon Brown wants us
to be happy, although no-one seems to know quite what
it means. A lady taxi driver I talked to had strong views
on the subject. Bringing up three teenage kids alone
meant 'happiness' was a luxury to her. That didn't stop
her being cheerful, if a touch cynical, on the subject.

HAVE you ever considered that some people are simply born happy, that happiness – or the ability to experience the feeling we call 'happy' – is in the genes?

Think of people you know. If your acquaintances are anything like mine, you'll be able to divide them quite easily into the happy ones and the miserable ones. But compare their lives and, when it comes down to it, there's probably not too much to choose between them. In fact, against all the odds, it's often the ones who have suffered the most who put the bravest face on things, who seem to get the most fun out of life, who seem 'happiest'.

Ask your friends and colleagues whether they consider themselves to be happy and I'll guarantee what their answer will be: "Yes, by and large, overall I would say I'm happy." What do they mean and what sort of happiness are they talking about? We ought to know because we set a lot of store by it these days.

If you believe the media and the self-improvement manuals, you'd think happiness was a 'right' – like the minimum wage and voting. Do the right things and it can be yours, too. Like winning a prize for good behaviour.

Alright, so you don't buy the 'reward' theory. Nor do I, so here's another idea. You know what gives you pleasure, don't you? Well, all you have to do is have more and more of the things you enjoy and you'll be happy. Right? Wrong.

Try this then. Love. After all, the Beatles famously told us "it's all we need" - as if we have this commodity in spades, to just dole out as much as we can, the more the merrier, and we'll get the benefit of being loved back. And then we'll be happy, won't we? I wish.

Is it wise to regard 'happiness' as a state? If anything, it's a feeling and not always long-lasting, either. It's certainly not a goal.

Here's another thing. Don't believe the songs. Thousands of them have contained the line "you make me happy." Er, no. Presuming the lyricist was referring to the experience of being 'in love' with another person, often if not always reciprocated, this is indeed heady stuff. But is it happiness? No, at least I hope not because we're not going to get much of that in a lifetime spanning three score years and ten, are we? Believe me, no-one can *make* you happy, however much they might want to.

There are a lot of things that give pleasure, excitement, satisfaction, elation or, simply, relief, that we can and do experience if we're lucky. Great food, great sex, love, friendship, travel, beauty, art, poetry, music, even winning, to name just a few, all give us pleasure – but none of them, individually or collectively, equate to 'being happy', not in any lasting sense, anyway.

How about giving birth to a child, raising a family, having grandchildren? Surely, we must be getting closer. Speaking personally, I have experienced great joy and been hugely moved by these most fundamental events in life but, and it's a big 'but', such rollercoasters of heightened emotion can go both up and down. Nature makes us no promises.

No, if we are searching for 'happiness' then the presumption is that if and when we find it, it will last. We have indeed come to believe, rightly or wrongly, that 'happiness' is a state of being and not just a temporary 'high'.

Where has this idea come from? Who has told us that out there somewhere, at the end of our personal rainbow, is that elusive 'pot of gold' we call happiness?

Religion, of course, has always dealt in punishment and reward. There's no middle ground between heaven and hell so we'd better shoot for the stars. Along with this goes the ancient notion that life is merely an earthbound journey towards a much greater goal. The Buddhist believes that earthly existence is a quest for the 'purer' state and even the more pragmatic Christian is taught that we are all born sinners and that the rest of our life is about self-improvement and striving to reach some state of 'goodness' where we will all be welcome to sit at God's right hand. Enticed by the proposition that our lives have a 'purpose' (whatever that may be), for generations we have struggled to comply. Work hard and apply yourself to the teachings of your cult or creed, and salvation, the state of nirvana - a place of complete bliss, delight and peace - will be yours to enjoy. Sounds pretty much like the pursuit of happiness, doesn't it?

The trouble is, as with all of evolution, we are currently at an in-between stage. Whilst we have long abandoned the notions of heaven and hell, redemption and salvation, we still cling to the thought that life is a quest although, deprived of the goals religion once provided, and having so far failed to come up with anything in their place, we have no idea what the purpose of such a quest might be. So, instead, we've substituted this wishy-washy idea that we are striving to 'be happy'.

The truth is that there are far more important things in life than being happy, things that we can deal with on a day-to-day basis, things that don't (or shouldn't) require us to sit around navel-gazing, searching for answers to questions we can't grasp. That's not to say there isn't a time and a place for reflection and contemplation, it's just that, for most of us, it's a luxury and there's an awful lot to be getting on with in the meantime, like earning a living and looking after the kids – which, to my mind, takes priority. And, if you're lucky, some of these things will give you pleasure along the way.

No-one in their right mind would claim that the process of bringing up a family, conducted over a period of twenty years or so, is a bundle of laughs. Of course not. Every parent will tell you it has its highs and lows. I know those who believe they've failed, who, in later life have seen their kids turn against them, blaming them for all that has gone wrong in their lives. But, for others, to come through it, to have made the difficult as well as the easy decisions, to have got the balance about right between encouragement, discipline, being soft and hard, and to see your kids turn out to be reasonably well-adjusted and secure human beings, well, I don't know anyone who looks back on that without a sense of immense satisfaction and fulfilment.

Satisfaction and fulfilment. I wonder if Mozart was concerned about being happy, or Leonardo or Shakespeare, or Einstein or Brunel. I doubt it. What they did care about, one suspects, was making the most of their gifts and talents to the enormous benefit of the rest of us. I like to think that these great men did get some joy from their lives, that when their time came they were able to look back knowing they had made a difference, and had left the world a better, richer, more enlightened place than it would have been without them.

To an extent that option is open to us all. It's tangible and achievable if we can only get away from the idea that unless we're enjoying ourselves every minute of every day, we must be doing something wrong. Life is a slow burn. It's a marathon, not a sprint. There's time for everything. But, it is also finite.

The one thing you can be sure of is that you're going to die. They used to call death 'the day of reckoning', when others, presumably from some higher place, would float above you as your spirit departed your mortal envelope, calculating the odds as to whether you'd made a reasonable hash of it all, or not.

To us this is not too helpful, simply because we have come to reject the idea of a celestial judge and jury assessing our lives retrospectively. Even the Victorian cameo of a family straining their ears to catch the last gasps of wisdom and advice at the bedside of an expiring patriarch is hard to take. Nowadays, rightly or wrongly, modern medicine makes sure that most people are well out of it by the time they depart this world.

Nevertheless, there is a lot to be said for regarding life as a long-term project. Real achievements are the ones that have taken time. Building a business, seeing an investment pay off, watching youngsters grow up, acquiring knowledge, learning a skill, appreciating great art. None of this happens overnight. It's the looking back on a job well done that provides the satisfaction, not to be compared with the enjoyment derived from a good meal out or unwrapping a gift.

Needless to say there are those who would disagree with any mention of achievement in the context of happiness.

I'm aware that 'achievement' tends to be a masculine word, not unlike 'success'. But that would be to see achievement in its narrowest sense, rather than against the broader backdrop of human endeavour. Anyone who sets out to do something and does it has 'achieved'. I have an elderly acquaintance who derives immense satisfaction every time she manages to complete a visit to the local shop. Beware anyone who offers her a well-meaning lift; they'll get a flea in the ear!

To genuinely help someone else is an important achievement, as is bringing fun and laughter into a room, not to mention bringing up a child. It follows that some sense of achievement is integral to reaching an overall state of contentment, which is as near as I can get to 'happiness'.

Whilst we're at it, let's lay another myth to rest. Does money bring happiness? No, of course it doesn't. Money or the lack of it is just one of many hurdles sent to try us as we attempt to navigate our way through the wilderness of life. Money, like sex, only preys on your mind if you're not getting it, so, if it's not to become an obsession, better to have enough rather than too little. The problem arises when you try to separate money from aspiration. What is enough for one person is too little for another and that's where unhappiness resides, not in the process of acquiring wealth, but in the disposing of it!

So, if happiness is an illusion and the real goal we should be setting ourselves is long-term contentment, how should we set about getting there?

Firstly, we have to assess our own potential – what we have to offer as individuals, what we can do that others can't or, at least, do as well if not better. This is the start point. Whether old or young, it's never too late to review where you are, how you've got there and where you might be going.

But, if this is to be a worthwhile exercise, there are two pre-conditions, firstly, to take responsibility for your past and present and, secondly, to set yourself realistic and *worthwhile* goals for the future.

This is a real problem with today's youngsters. There is absolutely no merit, for example, in aiming to be a millionaire by the time you are thirty if you haven't the faintest idea what you will do with the money if and when you've made it. This ill-considered, half-cock ambition will not lead to contentment, more likely to frustration and despair.

If, on the other hand, in your estimation, you need to be a millionaire to provide a secure future for your family, a good education for your kids and a pleasant environment in which to live, that is a different matter. In that case work out how you're going to do it - preferably engaged in something you're good at and will enjoy - and go for it.

Similarly, there is no point in deciding that you want to play football for England simply because you'd like to marry someone like Posh Spice and become famous. Unless, that is, you have shown signs from an early age of having extraordinary potential (which others will certainly have noticed). You may, on the other hand, have a great love of sport and want to work in the sports industry, or become a sports teacher. That's sensible and more likely to happen – and, who knows, you might still go on to be famous!

You see, ambition is just another way of describing expectations and more people become miserable and depressed because their expectations aren't realised than for any other reason. Therefore, to set yourself objectives that you are never going to realise is inviting failure and unhappiness.

Balance, balance, balance. It's extraordinary how much satisfaction can result from completing a simple task. I could give you examples galore – filling in a form, getting shot of an irritating chore, cooking a good omelette – hardly great achievements but it can feel as if they are!

So, identify modest, worthwhile objectives, ones you are likely to achieve, remembering, of course, that what is modest to you may be ambitious to someone else.

Finally, take a leaf out of Mozart's book, and set your sights on leaving the world a better place than you found it. This may seem grandiose, even implausible. But, it needn't. Everything is relative and to look outwards beyond oneself does not require the mind of a genius.

Oh, and there's one other thing. You'll never be happy if you have a guilty conscience. Keeping your slate as clean as possible will stand you in good stead. Ladies, particularly, avoid saying 'sorry' all the time and, gentlemen, don't behave as if you are carrying the worries of the whole world on your shoulders. Not all of the time anyway.

When all is said and done, what you make of your life comes down to an attitude of mind. Whatever happiness is, one thing is sure, you make your own. It's in your head so keep it clear.

If your parents are still alive and still married – you are amongst a rare minority even in the western world

Stress

*Stress goes with the job. You'd have to be superhuman
to sit in traffic day in day out without occasionally giving
in to a spot of road rage. Especially with an impatient
and probably equally stressed client in the back...*

WHEN you think what the cave men went through, it makes
you wonder whether we have a realistic attitude to stress.
Nowadays it's fashionable to blame it for just about everything
that can possibly go wrong with our minds and bodies. Well,
I don't blame stress, I blame the fact that we have forgotten
how to cope with it.

If you live in the real world, you're going to get stressed
- maybe not all the time, but often enough. It's when we
start regarding stress as the cause of our problems that we
run into trouble. Especially if we buy the idea that stress is
inflicted upon us by others and is an infringement of our
'rights'. It happens in court all the time, people making
hugely exaggerated claims for compensation because someone
(usually their manager at work) has caused them stress. It's
difficult to see the logic of this. It's like saying there should
never be disagreements or arguments. How can you employ
and manage people, let alone strive to get the best out of them,
without subjecting them to stress? Not to mention settling
a dispute in a court of law, the most stressful experience

imaginable! Funny how all those delicate, stress-damaged victims can't wait to get up before of a judge.

Normal people create and deal with stress all the time. Bringing up your children properly can be stressful for them and for you. The very acts of striving to do well, defending your principles, resisting a bully, protecting a loved one, getting to a meeting on time - all are perfectly normal, justifiable and stressful. Any harm done? I doubt it.

To an extent we can control how much stress we expose ourselves to, especially if we know what upsets us in the first place. Which varies from person to person. Take men and women. Most men can't believe the things that stress out their partners – and, needless to say, vice versa. Then there are those who look for trouble at every opportunity and seem to thrive on the stress they create. We all know someone like that. If in doubt, watch 'Big Brother'.

Others deliberately go into highly stressful occupations, such as the police or the armed services, although some still end up complaining about stress further down the line. Yes, I have great sympathy with the appalling situations that these people have to face, but surely they must know what lies in store? If not, then the recruiting sergeants are misleading these youngsters. Not a pleasant thought but not impossible either.

If, however, you are the other way inclined, you might think you could avoid stress altogether by never venturing beyond your front door. You'd be wrong. I know people who are so frightened of stress they live like hermits, avoiding normal day-to-day life at all costs. As it transpires they still get stressed but for different reasons, like what will happen to them if they don't see anyone from one week to the next or how will they make ends meet.

No, stress is unavoidable. What matters is how you deal with it.

Increasingly we are asked to believe that stress is a medical condition rather than merely a physical one. So be it. For all I know stress may well cause high blood pressure, raise cholesterol levels, cause hardening of the arteries and indigestion, plus a whole range of other symptoms. But then so might watching a cup final or placing a bet on a horse.

Stress exists for a reason, and a very good one at that. Nature has cleverly provided that when threatened or required to perform beyond our normal capacity, a sudden rush of adrenaline changes the way our bodies behave. We quite literally 'change modes'. Our heartbeat quickens, re-directing blood to satisfy the more pressing requirements of the brain and the muscles and putting on hold the non-urgent bodily functions such as digestion. As a result the mind becomes focussed and the body experiences a burst of energy and strength. This is why a mother finds the strength within her to lift a car off her child and a mountaineer can cling to a ledge with his fingertips. Of course, such extreme feats are only temporary and put enormous strain on the human structure. But they can also be immensely empowering and life-changing. This miraculous process is triggered by stress. So, don't knock it!

It's probable there are different types of stress, some more damaging than others. In the workplace, for example, the stress induced by having to get something done on time is quite different from worrying about whether the young turk down the corridor is after your job. The reason's clear enough – you can do something about meeting a deadline whereas worrying about something that might never happen and, anyway, is totally beyond your control, is fruitless. People who choose to throw themselves out of an aircraft subject themselves to horrendous stress but know that by pulling the ripcord at the right moment they will save their life. They're in control. Sitting on a 747 getting stressed because you are frightened it will crash just eats away at your insides. Healthy stress and unhealthy stress.

Nor is stress the same as fear. Worry is different again. Stress is running the mind and body at full stretch, like throttling your BMW up to full speed on an autobahn – you may be testing the engineering to breaking point but you won't harm the car. Neither is fear in itself damaging. We have evolved over hundreds of thousands of years to cope with it. It's part of our make up. Why else would people go to see horror films, terrify themselves at fairgrounds or get involved in extreme sports? An occasional rush of adrenaline is harmless, may even be therapeutic, keeping our systems ticking over. That's fear.

But it is possible, even likely, that constant fretting can make you ill. Worry is pointless. If you can't do something about it, don't waste time going there. And yet worry is a very human quality, endearing even, rooted in our underlying insecurity and lack of self-belief. 'He's a worrier,' we say, sympathetically, knowing there's absolutely nothing we can do to help. Worry is like a dripping tap, wastefully leaking away that precious adrenaline. A tap you can't turn off.

So, if we can't escape stress, can we get better at living with it? Yes, but firstly we have to get used to it. It won't go away. Secondly, we have to stop looking around for someone to blame. Like happiness, how you react to stress is in your own hands. It's tempting to blame others but, in the end, it's 'not their fault'. Lastly, we shouldn't be frightened of it. One of the benefits of getting older is learning what you can cope with and what you can't, it's part of our quest for self-knowledge and, ultimately, self-respect. Like everything else, dealing with stress – even turning it to our advantage - takes practice and you don't get any practice by running away from it.

Please, let's not take it too seriously when they tell us that stress is a 'bad thing'. It isn't. It's essential to the human condition and we have been provided with all the necessary tools to handle it.

Lastly, let's keep stress out of the courts. Along with a lot else in our burgeoning 'compensation' culture, stress has no business being there whatever the doctors and lawyers might say. They have a vested interest.

When all's said and done, would you want to live in a world without stress? How boring that would be.

Don't get stressed; it's not going to happen.

"1,000 police officers are off work every day with stress-related sickness costing taxpayers more than £1million a week."

DOCUMENTS OBTAINED UNDER THE FREEDOM
OF INFORMATION ACT, FEBRUARY, 2007

The Consumer Society

Maybe taxis are part of the consumer society. If so, you wouldn't think so talking to the men and women who drive them.

WE know well enough the benefits of living in a materialistic world. But, do we know what we are missing, what price we are paying for the 'privilege' of enjoying instant access to everything we want, as well as the means to afford it?

Our relentless march towards the kind of consumer society we are now a part of has been the inevitable consequence of an industrial revolution, followed by an unprecedented explosion in technology which, quite apart from anything else, has made our planet a very small place indeed.

The result is a population who regard work as a means to an end and wealth as the passport to an exciting new world of 'owning' and 'having', a world unimaginable to our grandparents half a century ago.

But with this abundance of riches on the one hand, comes the danger of deprivation on the other. For with the ability to buy everything we could possibly want, so the necessity to do things for ourselves recedes.

Why learn to play the piano and sing when you can buy a CD? Why learn how to cook when you can watch someone else doing it on television and then go out and buy it all ready prepared? Why go to a football match when you can see it from the equivalent of the director's box in the comfort of your own front room? And why limit your access to any of this when you can afford to write down the cost in the 'essentials' column of your household accounts?

In today's developed countries pretty much everything is readily available at a price we can afford. As demand has increased so has supply; prices have come down and, even in those cases where an item might still be beyond our means were it to be produced locally, you'll find it on the shelf, flown in, at a price that may seem absurdly low.

The Internet is stuffed full of bargains and, of course, air transportation means that you can order things from the other side of the world and still have them in your possession in the time it used to take to order from a supplier in your High Street. That's how it is now, imagine what life will be like in twenty, even ten, years time.

Of course, with all of this on tap, and so much to tempt us into becoming serial shoppers, we need more and more money to participate. That means longer working hours and generally less time and energy to relax and enjoy the fruits of our labours. There's the paradox, here's the question: is the promise of the consumer society true or false? False, because what has got lost in this chase for material gain is the realisation that there is much more to life than possession.

Our grandparents knew this. They had no choice in the matter. If they didn't entertain themselves, no-one would. If they couldn't cook they'd starve and if they wanted to watch football, the only way was to go to the ground and buy a ticket. This meant that they acquired a whole range of skills and habits, which, fifty years on, aided by a hyperactive welfare state, we don't need. It would be no contradiction in terms to say that their reality was different to ours.

Why does this matter? *Because in our infinitely richer world, we run the risk of leading a poorer life.*

Rubbish, you might say. Anyone who wants to learn to cook or to play the piano or to paint has more opportunity to do so than ever before. Quite right. But for opportunities to be worth anything they have to be taken up. If they're not, they will surely disappear. Supply and demand, the very bedrock of the consumer society.

The fear is that we will move on and forget.

I hate the idea that people are working their rocks off just to earn money. As we've moved forward it would be gratifying to think that more and more of us have the chance to discover the best of what life has to offer – art, literature, music, travel (by which I don't mean travelling to other countries and getting drunk in fake English pubs).

It is these elements in life that fire our imaginations, enable us to grow, to explore and extend the limits of our instincts and feelings. Our imaginative and emotional development is not enhanced by ownership but by experience and, whilst you can buy the chance to experience something, you can't buy the experience itself.

If that sounds a bit much, let's cut it down to size. I'm a great sports fan but what attracts me is not whether my team wins or loses but the titanic struggle that is often part of the process.

I like sportsmen. They exist at the cutting edge of human endeavour, often battling with the elements as well as with each other. I admire the single-mindedness of champions, their quest for perfection, their desire to be the best and the fact that they have nowhere to hide. They either cut it or they don't. Ultimately, this is the stuff of greatness and we recognise it when we see it.

Sadly, the sporting arena is one of the few places left where we can enjoy such emotion. Heroism is in short supply. Of course, you could argue that professional sport is one of the least commendable manifestations of the consumer society. We pay young men obscene sums of money to kick a ball around which they subsequently spend disgracefully in the full glare of publicity. But this is missing the point. It's not the money inherent in the modern game that intrigues; it's the spiritual hike we get from watching it. The cash merely demonstrates how highly we value the experience.

Consumerism has led to other problems, too.

Living in a society where everything is driven by low prices has eroded choice, not increased it - precisely the opposite of what the so-called 'free' market promised to do. Mrs Thatcher believed that increased competition would *always benefit the consumer.* She was wrong. It might work in the States, where they have a market six times the size of ours, but it doesn't work here.

I'll give you some examples of why every economist since the war has been wrong on this point.

The railways. Broadcasting. The postal service. Power. Directory enquiries. Spot the connection between these apparently totally different things? You've got it, they are all businesses that were once monopolies, 'owned' or regulated by the government.

Now, look what's happened in each case.

It must have seemed obvious to our parents that a national railway service was a good idea – a railway network designed to cover every nook and cranny of the UK with lower volume routes subsidised by the more profitable metropolitan lines. In fact, this in itself was a consolidation of what had gone before when the original railways had been divided up into separate companies each serving a segment of the UK. Still,

British Railways worked. Bearing in mind the complexity of rail travel, the different sorts of services required for different areas of the country, British Railways became a bit of a national treasure preserving the traditions, and indeed culture, of the grand age of steam.

Then along came Dr Beeching in the '60's, charged with the unenviable task of closing down small rural sidelines in the pursuit of lower fares and greater efficiency. The result? Many areas of the countryside became isolated and dependent upon the motorcar. This set the precedent for privatisation in the 80's which led to the absurd idea that one company could own the tracks whilst others ran the trains – a recipe for disaster than any management student worth his salt could have predicted! A sure guarantee that no-one would ever again take responsibility for anything that went wrong, the tragic outcome of which we have seen more than once since. Meanwhile, prices have rocketed and services got worse.

It seems pretty sensible to have a national postal service, too, doesn't it? A service that everyone can trust, understand and buy in to. Until recently this is what we had. Of course, a 'national' postal service did not necessarily need to be 'nationalised' – you'll have gathered by now that I am not in favour of the Government running anything - still, it worked pretty well. Postmen wore the same uniforms, post boxes were red and charges were the same throughout the system. What's more, by and large, the mail got through safely and reliably. Then the government decided that it would be in the interest of the consumer to 'privatise' the Post Office because this would lead to greater competition, lower prices and greater efficiency. What happened? The opposite. In the sudden pursuit of 'profits' and manned by a group of senior managers who had never had to deliver 'profits' in their life, costs went up and efficiency went down.

Competition had little or no effect and all that de-nationalisation achieved was to destroy the values and practices that had existed before. Nowadays, postmen re-post letters because they aren't paid to do overtime and what's left of the Post Office (or whatever it is now called) has no alternative but to seek contracts and markets overseas to generate a 'bottom line' when, previously, it's sole raison d'être was to run a domestic postal service second to none in the world. Oh, and don't believe that the Post Office is in trouble because of e-mailing and the computer, it was on the slippery slope long before that.

Electricity and gas have faired no better. I still can't understand how a system that uses the same pipelines and cables, not to mention the same suppliers, can offer the consumer genuinely lower prices? Well, I can - because I've taken the trouble to find out. Here it is. The savings are in the cost of administration. Lower bills mean the company employs fewer people to prepare them. Never mind quality of service, if you change your supplier from British Gas to Powergen, what you are doing is moving from a well-staffed and resourced company to one that isn't. That's how the money is saved! Brilliant! Well done, government. Of course, in the end, British Gas becomes so run down by having to compete in this stupidly regulated system that it becomes weakened to the point it becomes a victim of a foreign takeover. At the same time Powergen has to invest in more resources to cope with demand so their prices go up. Game, set and match. Note that 'regulation' never goes away, it just changes its shirt depending upon the political playing field of the day.

Let's finish with Directory Enquiries, the most ridiculous example of all. For years we had a perfectly good system operated by British Telecom. You dialled 192 and a helpful operator (who spoke English) told you what you wanted to know for a very reasonable set price. It worked. Now, what do we have? Dozens of services, all offering the same thing, providing an unremarkable service at a higher price! I can't even remember their numbers anymore! Can you honestly say the consumer is better off?

Not only this, but the amount of paperwork and administration in the home required to keep track of all this 'choice' is frightening. It's worth twenty quid a month not to have to do it!

Why has all this gone wrong, why were the politicians so misguided? I'll tell you. This country is *too small for all this 'free market' stuff.*

You see, it might work in America, which is where all consumerist thinking originated, but it doesn't work here. Well, that's not quite true. It will work here in a manner of speaking because market forces always do. The tragedy is that we lose out in this slavish pursuit of a 'free' market.

I don't particularly like monopolies, but I have come to the conclusion that we need them, at least some of the time. If you want the best in a small country like ours, you have to let a few businesses have theirs market pretty much to themselves.

I've mentioned some of them. Another prime example is broadcasting – do you really think the BBC would have been able to produce all those expensive period dramas if it had had six or seven other national broadcasters breathing down its neck? They only had to compete with ITV – and it worked! There isn't, and never was, enough money in the system for more than that. Now we're suffering the consequences of too much competition.

At one level the public don't really care. The fact that they've tolerated Auntie BBC for so long is because she generally turns up with the goods. No amount of arguing about the politics of public broadcasting or the rights and wrongs of the license fee will change things. But if the quality of the programming deteriorates, then another great national institution begins to go the way of the lemmings.

Similarly with British Rail, the Post Office, Directory Enquiries and for that matter Telecom. The public did not want or ask for dozens of telephone companies, the whole process was driven by political dogma, commercial incompetence and lack of vision.

The consumer society has within it the seeds of its own destruction. It is not necessarily about increased choice and lower prices across the board (as Mrs Thatcher was fond of saying). Choice works vertically and horizontally – you can have a surfeit of virtually identical products at varying prices whilst, at the same time, lose other genuinely alternative products entirely. For example, if you want to stay in a five-star hotel, it's no consolation having a hundred b&b's competing for your custom if the only good hotel in town has closed down.

Of course, you might ask why anyone would want to stay in a five-star hotel when there are perfectly good bed and breakfasts available. But that's not economics, that's politics.

No, if you get it wrong, as we have, blind faith in the consumer society will lead to far less choice at much higher prices.

That's where we're heading and I don't like it.

The personal debt mountain (in the UK) is increasing by £1million every four minutes. Total personal debt stands at £1.278billion.

STUDY OF BANK OF ENGLAND DATA BY THE MONEY
EDUCATION CHARITY CREDIT ACTION, JANUARY 2007

Retirement

According to industry experts, income from pension plans has collapsed by nearly 80% over the last ten years. All self-employed people wonder what's in store for them further down the line and, not surprisingly, it's a favourite topic up for discussion during a cab ride.

THE question is whether we shall ever be able to look forward to retirement again. That is 'retirement' in the sense that our parents understood the word. Unless, of course, you work for the government, which, presumably, more and more people will now want to do.

For the rest of us, the picture looks pretty bleak.

Why has the pensions system collapsed? Principally because the Chancellor of the Exchequer has taxed it out of existence. We're now at a stage where the average employee in the private sector will have to work until he's sixty-seven in order to be able to retire on a half decent pension whilst his contemporary working for the state will be able to retire at sixty-five (sixty in some cases) on an index-linked state pension underwritten by the taxpayer. Take MP's, for example. Earlier this year they voted themselves a £168million gold-plated pension scheme plus a new 'communications allowance' which will cost taxpayers a further £6million a year. They now have one of the most generous pension packages around, so much so that an MP retiring today after 26 years service would collect an inflation proof £40,000 a year! Ironic that at a time when the public have become totally disillusioned with their performance and behaviour, politicians should be lining their pockets for their old age.

If the Chancellor *really* wanted to re-build pensions in the private sector, the first thing he would do is remove the onerous burden of taxation that he put there in the first place. Not difficult. So, why doesn't he do it?

It is almost impossible *not* to believe that there is another agenda at work. Either the Chancellor and his political cronies are plain stupid or they have a plan, namely, that more and more people will opt to work directly or indirectly for the government at the expense of the private sector. As this process really begins to bite over the next ten or twenty years, we shall see an increasing volume of the work currently in the hands of private, wealth-creating companies being taken over by the state. In other words, more government control, more centralism, a new wave of 'nationalisation' and less likelihood that any of these 'new' public employees will ever again enjoy the freedom of voting for any alternative political party.

Yet again we see New Labour's 'centre right' paying lip-service to their 'partnership' with the private sector whilst their 'left-wing' colleagues at the Treasury and in Whitehall systematically destroy it.

Fortunately, this is unlikely to work for two reasons.

Firstly, by definition you can't talk about pensions without setting a pretty long timescale and there is every chance that at some point in the next half century, the electorate will realise that creeping socialism is not what it wants and, secondly, that with the working culture changing, people will not actually want to 'retire' anyway.

Let's think for a moment about retirement and what it really means. Firstly, it's a relatively recent phenomenon. Prior to the industrial revolution few had occupations they could 'retire' from. Families who'd worked on the land for all their lives never retired. Each generation followed in the footsteps of the last providing and maintaining the family's standard of living as parents and grandparents became too old to perform the tasks required. 'Retirement' came neither through choice nor at some pre-determined point in time, but through infirmity. This is still the case in many rural communities throughout the west and, indeed, almost entirely in the third world.

It was only when offices and factories started to employ an increasing proportion of the working population that we saw the introduction of defined working hours and places of work, which required long journeys from home. A much more rigid framework of employment emerged and 'A fair day's work for a fair day's pay' became the maxim for a new generation of manual and white-collar workers.

In this way the working day became clearly delineated from time at home and people became used to the idea of 'going to work' and the regime that went with it. Instead of Nature calling the shots as in a predominantly agricultural economy, so it became the employers, the factory owners, shopkeepers, 'professional' firms, banks and institutions.

'Working' came to mean selling your services to the employer. 'Retirement' meant not having to do it anymore.

Those of you who travel to work by train will be aware that there are always at least half a dozen people in the carriage working out their time until retirement. "Only another three years," you'll hear them say, "and then it's retirement to that little thatched cottage in Swanage," or whatever other remote beauty spot they've had earmarked for their final chapter.

It sounds like a dream, doesn't it? Well, for the best part of this century it's been a dream, which, extraordinarily, has come true for millions of people. But, it would seem, not for much longer. Regrettable though that may be, we have to come to terms with the fact that the pensions industry has been underpinned by an unprecedented period of economic growth and reasonably good fiscal planning, a period that has now come to an end.

In my experience retirement is not straightforward anyway. What do people expect - that up to and including that long-awaited Friday they'll be doing something they don't like anymore and then, the following Monday, suddenly everything will be wonderful? Not to mention that the old salary cheques will be magically swapped for monthly payments from an anonymous insurance company. In other words, everything will stay much the same without having to go to work.

If only that was all there was to it!

Problem number one - what does the other half have to say about it? Of course, it could happen either way, but speaking on behalf of the half dozen chaps I know who have been through the experience, not one of them anticipated that whilst life might be changing dramatically for them, their wife had a well-oiled existence of her own which she had no intention of changing!

This really does catch them out. I suppose it's pretty obvious that most working partners don't spend much time worrying about what their other half gets up to while they're in the office nine til five. To a working couple, it comes as a bit of a shock to discover that, simply because the time has come for one half to dramatically change their life, the other may not want to. Or, in the case of a non-working wife, that, with the kids long gone, she has her own circle of friends, diary of activities and events that has kept her perfectly happy during his office hours for a number of years.

Someone once told me that when a man first retires he'll start out by asking his wife why she's going out, a few weeks later he'll be asking what time she'll be back and then, after a month or so, whether he can go, too. Well, many a true word spoken in jest. I've seen them at the supermarket.

It's a vulnerable time, particularly for a man. A sudden and dramatic drop in self-esteem invariably accompanies the loss of a job albeit through 'retirement'. The man who for years thought he was indispensable will be shocked to discover that the 'phone isn't ringing with queries from anxious ex-colleagues seeking his counsel on every topic from where to find the stapler to handling a difficult client. When you're used to being needed, it comes as a deflating surprise to discover you're not anymore, even worse that you might never have been in the first place.

After years of working amongst a team of people (okay some of them may have driven you to distraction), being home alone with nothing to do can be traumatic. Good for neither brain nor body. I've known men who've died soon after retiring, others who grieve over their lost job at a time in their life when they'd imagined they would feel on top of the world. As for all those 'hobbies' they were going to take up, not to mention the travel and the Open University degree, well, when it actually comes to it...

Even assuming that you've come through the process with your dignity intact and some renewed interest in life and, if you're lucky, a bit of cash, dangers lie ahead. If you've been successful at accumulating money, how good are you at managing it? I've known at least two people who have spent a lifetime earning their modest wealth only to blow the lot. Why? In the main, they got bored. So they got involved in some 'investment' opportunity which they would have run a mile from in their working years, or, started a 'little business' – it might be an antique shop, or a restaurant or something to do with water filters – just to keep their mind occupied. Needless to say, the fact that they'd never actually run a business before didn't deter them, but it cost them dear just the same. Where are those damned professional advisers when you need them? Don't worry, they're there alright, only too pleased to relieve you of some of your hard earned cash in exchange for the same advice you'd get for nothing from a bank or building society or, better still, from a slightly older acquaintance who has already been there and done it.

It shouldn't be like this.

So let's try to see things differently. Life is a series of chapters and it helps if we can progress to the next one smoothly. Certainly, it would be agreeable if there was a point in one's life - be it at forty, fifty, sixty, seventy - when you didn't *have* to work anymore, not in order to live reasonably comfortably, that is. It doesn't mean you have to stop working. There are plenty of jobs that do not involve getting paid and maybe this is how we shall have to regard 'retirement' in the future.

Of course, one man's meat is another man's poison and no two individuals will agree on what is an acceptable and affordable standard of living. But, sooner or later, sure as eggs are eggs, we all have to settle for something.

You wouldn't think it was that difficult, but it defeats a surprisingly large number of people. Part of the problem is that employment itself is a poor environment within which to make such choices. Why? Because at precisely the time we should be thinking about the future, our jobs are often at they're most demanding, embroiling us in the present.

Nevertheless, it is a good idea to think these things through early enough to exercise some control over the timing and manner of your departure from full-time employment rather than wait until the decision is forced upon you. The younger you are, the easier it is to adjust to a radical change of lifestyle. My father grafted his way up to a senior position in a company where he'd worked for forty years. When he was sixty they asked him to take early retirement on a reduced pension. Why, I don't know. What I do know is that he never got over the shock of what he saw as a betrayal. He had always assumed that he would go when it suited him. He was wrong and learned too late that companies don't have feelings.

It helps to have some idea what you intend to do with the immense amount of time you will suddenly have on your hands. Of course, it may be better to ease your way out, either by working fewer days a week or switching to some kind of consultancy basis, but these options are not open to many.

So, what's it to be? Firstly don't fall for the clichés. The cottage in Swanage would be great if it wasn't for the fact that all those locals who made such a fuss of you when you went down for a holiday, suddenly don't want to know you as a full-time neighbour. Anyway, you'll soon start yearning for the friends and family you've left back in suburbia, not to mention the fact that the children and grandchildren don't pop down every other weekend as you'd always imagined they would. In fact, even a move of a few miles can be enough to put paid to regular contact with the friends and acquaintances you've taken for granted for twenty years or more. In fact, I can never understand why people uproot themselves at precisely the point in their lives when they need their friends and family around them. But they do.

Hobbies aren't necessarily the answer. You may have always wished you could play the piano, paint portraits or play golf off single figures, but, frankly, the chances of achieving any kind of proficiency at something new when you're past sixty is remote and the frustrations of failure can bring more pain than pleasure.

You may be luckier if retirement offers you the chance to concentrate greater time and effort on a subject that has interested you previously and for which you may even have demonstrated some talent. I have a friend who has successfully qualified as a wine judge at the age of sixty and now travels all over the country (and gets paid) for expressing his views and opinions on something he loves. The time to get involved in other interests is before you give up work, not afterwards.

Believing that you will spend your retirement travelling all over the world can be a disappointment, too. Unless you have a real taste for it, and preferably some experience, long-haul travel is an expensive and harassing experience, not necessarily well suited to those who are newly retired on a fixed income.

I've already touched on the hazards of starting businesses and making investments. Beware the 'grass is greener' syndrome. Other people's businesses are seldom easier than the one you've been used to, even though they may have appeared to be from outside. Similarly, just because you've been bossed around for years does not mean that running your own show is a bed of roses by comparison. You are likely to get a few nasty surprises and discover that your old boss had more on his mind than you ever realised.

No, all this retirement stuff needs to be considered much earlier than most of us get round to. In a sentence, ease yourself into it, preferably over a period of time, with a realistic view of what you might do to improve the quality of your life by the time R-Day finally arrives.

Assuming, of course, that any of us are given the chance to retire at all.

Official figures show that Britain's 'grey' workforce - pension-aged employees still working - has increased by more than 200,000 in the last two years. There are currently nearly 1.2 million workers over retirement age.

The Future

*Can we affect the future for the benefit of the generations
who will follow us? Are greenhouse gasses and global
warming the real issues that confront us? Or could it
be that for the last two centuries Mother Nature has
been kind and allowed us to live a charmed life?*

FOR the last half-century or so we've assumed that things
will move forward steadily, free of too many major man-
made or natural disasters, towards a better, more stable and
peaceful future. Indeed, the overwhelming thrust of most
governments and politicians throughout the world has been
towards this end, whatever their shortcomings, and however
misguided some of their methods. Broadly speaking, in the
west at any rate, we have seen just such a process unfold and
there aren't many who would disagree that the world is a
better place today than it was in 1950.

As a result we have become used to the idea that somehow,
allowing for the odd setback, things will continue to get better
rather than worse in the future.

The question is: why do we make such an assumption?

The answer exposes both a fallacy and a folly, namely,
our belief that the future is down to us – what *we* make of
things, how *we* manage to control and check our excesses,
even how *we* control the environment.

The trouble is we don't. As the recent alarming series of natural disasters has reminded us, *we* are a very small force indeed when pitted against the unlimited resources and power of nature.

In fact, it's surprising that nature has been so gentle with us in recent times. History may show that we have lived a charmed life during a period of time when nature has been so benign it has allowed us to thrive and prosper to an unprecedented extent, so much so that we have come to believe that we command all we survey.

For mankind to prosper and make progress is not too difficult so long as Nature stays her hand. What happens when her fury is unleashed paints a rather different picture. We've seen it all in recent times. The devastating effect of floods, hurricanes, earthquakes and eruptions, reducing even the most civilised and richest countries to despair - not to mention the incalculable cost of replacing what was there before. People picking themselves up, rebuilding their homes and lives in the belief that catastrophe couldn't possibly strike in the same place twice.

How many times can humans suffer such setbacks? How long does it take for morale to sink so low that they can't be bothered to build new homes, let alone paint them? How often can governments find the funds to re-construct whole communities, replace the infrastructure and fabric of towns and cities built up over hundreds of years, yet destroyed in minutes?

If all this sounds like a prophecy of doom, just think for a second. The balance of nature rests on a knife-edge and that balance is shifting as you read this. Global warming *is* changing the climate, there *is* more warm water in the seas, more rain in the mountains, more violent winds threatening whole swathes of the world where more temperate weather has existed for most of our lifetimes and those of our parents. And if you believe that we can cure all this by legislating against the use of pollutants and CFC's, well, you have more faith in the scientists than I do. It turns out after years of pronouncing the opposite that rain forests actually increase global warming rather than prevent it! Just one example of why we shouldn't take the 'experts' too seriously.

Even a marginal increase in the frequency and severity of natural disasters would put an immense strain on our species – both emotionally and economically. Wars are bad enough but at least we can do something to stop them if we have the will. Not so with natural disasters.

In the UK our moderate weather pattern is largely due to the gulf stream, a current of warm sea and air which makes its way across the Atlantic from South America, quite literally 'bathing' us in warmth despite our latitude which otherwise would bring us a colder, more typically northern climate. What happens to the gulf stream is not determined somewhere just off the coast of Cornwall, but thousands of miles away in a part of the world where, in recent times, there has been a significant and measurable climatic change. We are not immune to potential disasters by any means.

Imagine living in a small mountain town in Italy, the kind of place you might choose to go for a fortnight's vacation, knowing that last winter there was a mudslide comprising half a mountainside of earth and debris which, moving at an alarming rate, stopped just short of your back door. And knowing that if the same record level of rainfall comes again next winter, your town and everything in it will be buried. This is happening now and Italy is not far away.

It seems unthinkable that anything of a similar nature could occur here, but it will. When that time comes we can only hope we're prepared, if only so that we are not taken entirely by surprise.

Of course we might be lucky and it won't happen, at least, not for a long time – let's be optimistic like the Italian mountainfolk, none of whom have yet left their homes to seek the safety of the valleys.

But it might not be such a bad idea to dwell on the fragility of our existence once in a while, if only to avoid the arrogance of thinking we control the environment.

It might also help us realise that life is a gift which we should make the most of on a daily basis. This is not to say we shouldn't dream and make plans, simply that we should make sure we enjoy the process of bringing them to fruition.

It's been said many times before, but life is not a rehearsal.

If you have food and a place to sleep with a roof you are richer than 75% of people in the world

The Thought Police

If you drive a cab for a living you're likely to get to know the Old Bill pretty well. Despite this, I've not met a taxi driver who doesn't think there should be more old-fashioned policing on the streets and less policy making behind closed doors.

HOW would you describe a police force that telephones you when you have committed no criminal offence and tells you that because you were heard to express a view that runs contrary to the 'message' of the political party in power, you should be very careful?

I would call them 'thought police'. Something we have not had in this country in living memory. No need to hold your breath any longer, George Orwell is with us right now.

If you didn't pick up this particular story in the press, a rather nice elderly couple asked their local council if they would be allowed to put some pro-Christian literature alongside the pro-gay leaflets in the reception of their local town hall. The next thing they knew the police sent officers to their home to warn them they were "walking on eggshells."

The same thing happened when an experienced broadcaster remarked on Radio Four that she had concerns about gay couples adopting little boys.

In both cases the police admitted that no criminal offence had taken place but that they were 'obliged' to investigate reports of potentially homophobic incidents.

In which case how and why did they get involved in the first place? You guessed it - because they received complaints, almost certainly from 'professionals' employed by the local council to monitor such things. Let's face it, this is a another new industry.

I have no doubt that in both cases the 'offenders' put their side of the argument concisely and well. After all, their views were neither particularly reactionary nor unusual, nor were they expressed in a violent context. The fact that we have a remarkable tolerance to homosexuality in this country, including the acceptance of civil marriages for gay couples, seems to have no bearing on the matter at all. Nor do I believe for a moment that gay people want others to be harassed for holding views which someone else has decided are counter to their cause.

So, what is driving this phenomenon? Namely, that not only is there a threat to our ancient and hard won right to express ourselves freely and peacefully on matters of reasonable concern, but that it is the police, so-called guardians of our liberty, who are doing the threatening?

There could be two reasons. Firstly, the present government has been quick to take on full time employees in the state sector to drive through its social policies, without any thought as to what might happen if they were successful. Most people would agree that the persecution of gays is intolerable. However, by the time the politicians got hold of the issue as a potential vote winner, the process of fully integrating gays into the community was well under way. In truth, it probably didn't require the government to do very much, if anything at all. By then the gay lobby had already achieved and exceeded it's objectives more quickly and comprehensively than it had ever dreamed possible. The character in "Little Britain", still protesting against his homophobic family and neighbours long after they have accepted him, is closer to the truth than many would choose to admit.

The problem is that we now have an army of 'outreach' workers and local council employees who are, to all intents and purposes, redundant. We know that there is no way this government will put state employees out to grass, so what we are left with is a myriad of busybodies, some well-meaning, some not, trying to justify their continuing employment. One obvious solution is to launch investigations and file complaints.

Nevertheless, any major social change leaves in its wake legitimate doubt and concern. By stifling the few remaining voices courageous enough to make themselves heard, you will, in the end, defeat the cause of tolerance rather than help it. If gay people allow themselves to be portrayed as victims when society no longer sees them as such, they will invite renewed parody and persecution. At another level, if gays are seen to be complicit in the suppression of free speech and the right of individuals to express their concerns and beliefs, then society will not quickly forgive them.

Here's another possibility - just a possibility - but one the conspiracy theorists amongst you will enjoy. Suppose the government really is intent upon restricting the rights of the individual to debate and criticise its actions? Wouldn't this be a perfect way to start, by promoting anti-free speech legislation as a way of protecting 'persecuted' minorities? I do hope that gay people, so recently and triumphantly 're-enfranchised', are not about to become a different kind of victim, namely, that they consciously or unconsciously allow themselves to be manipulated by politicians in the cause of dumbing down.

The fact that the police allow themselves to become embroiled in all this is short sighted, pathetic and outrageous. Anyone who has tried and failed to get the police to investigate a domestic theft or some other crime will find no consolation in the knowledge that 'potentially homophobic incidents' attract police time and attention with terrifying immediacy.

Matters of great importance are at stake.

PS Did you know the police have been voted "Number One Employer of Gays", just ahead of IBM. One in six employees of the Police Force are gay, double the percentage of gays in the overall population.

Residents in a London street reported a sudden increase in burglaries. The Police responded by putting up signs saying 'Burglars Operate in this Area'

Sex

*It had to rear its head eventually, although in my experience
this is not a subject often discussed between drivers
and passengers - more often between the passengers
themselves. But then, think what cab drivers overhear...*

IT may be that this generation is the first to finally separate
out the three aspects of sex and understand each in isolation
from the others, namely, gratification, passion and love. In the
process we may have created a three-headed monster capable
of triggering the decline and fall of western civilisation.

If that sounds overstated, let me remind you there are
many historians who still believe sexual depravity and moral
corruption brought down many a great civilisation in the
past. Imagine the scene: an orgy of jaded, half-naked ex-
imperialists, eating, drinking and fornicating themselves into
a stupour, while the heroic invader bursts in, brandishing the
sword of virtue!

Whether this ever actually happened is another matter,
but it's a colourful thought. Every dog has its day and as one
generation relaxes to enjoy the spoils of its triumphs, the next
is waiting in the wings to take over.

So, where exactly does sex fit into this cycle of conquest
and defeat?

Well, one theory is that as people become richer so they become lazier, more dissatisfied with materialism and inclined to experiment increasingly with mind-altering experiences – in a nutshell, sex, drugs and rock n' roll. The trouble is these pastimes are not likely to do much for physical fitness, let alone the will to fight!

Of course, sex has always terrified the ruling classes who, whether they are kings, bishops or politicians, have considered they should have a monopoly of fleshly pursuits whilst denying the same to their subjects. Why, because gratification, passion and love are distracting, disruptive, time-consuming and potentially harmful. Certainly, insofar as it usually involves upwards of two people, coitus has the potential to damage and corrupt. Equally, there are still those amongst us who would maintain that sex practised alone is deeply harmful. More later.

In any event there is no doubt that sex, at its best beautiful and life-enhancing, can also be grubby and degrading. Where to draw the line, then? How to maximise the good and minimise the bad?

Let's get back to those three ingredients: gratification, passion and love. Taken together, it is hard to think of a more perfect union of forces gifted to us by nature for us to explore and revel in. Separately they may not be harmful, but can be.

On the face of it, nature is only interested in procreation and the survival of our species. But, why passion and love? Indeed, what are they? So familiar have they become, so recognisable when they hit us, that we seldom stop to think.

Firstly, let's see what we know about passion. It would appear to be the driving force behind great art, music, poetry, sport, not to mention the pursuit of power and wealth. All great achievers have it in spades, in fact, it's hard to imagine how anyone can truly excel in any sphere of human endeavour without it. Passion, then, is powerful; a combination of drive, inspiration, energy, willpower, often courage, coupled with a fierce knowledge of what you want and the almost unlimited appetite to go out and get it.

Gratification, although similarly compulsive, is rather less to do with our human side, more to do with the animal. Sexual gratification in particular has been put there by nature to make sure that, at the most basic level, we seek to relieve the 'itch' of frustration, predominately with a member of the opposite sex, in order to guarantee that sufficient eggs get fertilised to generate new lives.

Love, in some respects the most mysterious of the three, is the mortar that bonds the whole. Quite literally, preventing relationships falling apart. Even at its most fundamental level, represented by friendship, caring and trust, love will surmount obstacles, overcome pain, repair damage and make forgiveness possible. It also provides the security and stability that nature intends children to have in order to reach their full potential as befits the most advanced species of life on the planet. Manifested throughout the world by the family unit – not an invention of man but pre-determined in our genes - a human embryo will not develop into a fully matured human being without a loving group to support it.

Now, it goes without saying that finding gratification, passion and love all in one package may take a little time. Again, nature has supplied us with the means. The pursuit of the young female by the male (or 'courting' as we rather charmingly used to call it) provides the opportunity to set about this complex task against a lengthy timescale in a more or less safe environment. To achieve this, over hundreds, thousands of years, throughout all cultures, we've put in place rituals, rules if you like, mainly within the family, and often under the guise of religious practice. These rituals, which include family meetings, dowries, social introductions, as well as a whole host of other checks and balances, have meant that couples have had the chance to get to know each other, to explore love and passion as well as gratification, so that by the time they are ready to settle down together and 'procreate', their relationship is cocooned and protected as far as possible against the ravages and dangers of day-to-day life.

Today all this is being undone by the burgeoning practice of recreational sex amongst young people.

Sex without emotional commitment is perfectly possible, even desirable under certain circumstances. But this is adult stuff requiring a maturity of mind and spirit, not to mention a relatively strong character and a secure state of mind.

Teenagers and others who have not yet reached this point in their emotional development can be extremely vulnerable when sex comes before love. If this sounds old-fashioned, let's explore the idea further. How often is that first sexual experience fulfilling? Think back. With a casual partner, and in the absence of love or passion, such a negative first experience may have disastrous consequences. It only requires one party to blame the other, or to be sarcastic or cruel, and it can take years for the wound to heal, if ever. Within a loving or even friendly, well-meaning relationship, such a setback can be easily accommodated, put down to experience with a view to a better result at the next attempt.

Psychologists will tell you that we are at our most mentally fragile when sexually aroused – indeed, Freud built a whole science around this theory. Get sex wrong and a whole host of scary mental associations can be triggered, many, if not all of them, likely to last for life.

It is known that rape, child abuse and violence, as well as many other unpleasant, repetitive traits and characteristics including murder, often have their roots in early, painful, sexual experience. We get it wrong at our peril.

There is absolutely nothing casual about sex, especially when emotionally immature youngsters are involved. Sex within a loving relationship makes sense for very sound reasons. Casual sex is for grown-ups and probably not as many of them as you think.

Is it possible for sex to come before love? Of course, we've all been there at some time or another. But don't forget the human psyche is subtle and sophisticated. Sexual attraction takes into account a whole range of factors, many of them unconscious. It's rare to experience the chemistry of physical attraction without the brain having already undertaken a sifting process designed to eliminate rank outsiders. Consequently, we are nearly always attracted to people with whom we could fall 'in love' under favourable circumstances.

Here's another point in favour of love. As time passes we come to rely on it more as passion and desire decline. It helps enormously if love was there in the first place! Even where couples experience the waning of the sex drive in different measures, one losing interest ahead of the other, these contradictions, and many others, can be absorbed within a loving partnership.

Sex can't do this. Not long ago I talked to a man whose wife had literally just walked out on him. He told me how hard it was for him to understand her leaving when they'd made love just the night before!

Our quest for eternal youth doesn't help. Personally, I'm all for growing old gracefully. Like most men, having had my brain located somewhere between my legs for most of my life, I can't wait for it to go back to where it belongs. We've come to accept it with women but when I see men going to ridiculous lengths to preserve their youth and virility, I ask why. You name it: drugs, cosmetic surgery, more intimate surgery, trophy mistresses, sex aids, dyed hair, toupees, funny exercises, inappropriate clothes, silly cars, they're up for it – anything other than admit that nature doesn't need them to sow their seed anymore. They're past it but won't, or can't, accept the fact.

Obviously solitary sex is not an acceptable option for them.

A golfing friend once said: "Your swing is like masturbation, you may get a great deal of pleasure from it but the rest of us find it disgusting!"

I was a bit upset at the time. Firstly, I thought my golf swing was OK, but, mainly, I was disappointed that anyone would find the thought of anyone engaging in an entirely private and harmless pastime to be in any way disgusting. A joke, yes, disgusting, no. In this day and age - well, I ask you?

Certainly, if we are to believe what we read and hear, everyone is doing it. So much so, that one of the great remaining taboos of our lifetime, namely, that girls do it, too, is now a matter for tabloid consumption. When there is public speculation about what object a contestant on a peak-time reality show will use to achieve orgasm, then I think we can safely assume that the subject is up for public debate – and family viewing, too.

It could be argued that solitary sex has a great deal to be said for it. It keeps the young off the streets, exercises their imagination and teaches them about their sexual responses whilst, in the case of the older generation, prevents extra-marital affairs and, I suspect, prostate and breast cancer. But I don't know that.

Which only leaves the perverse and depraved, which is where we came in. Like all physical functions, the sexual appetite can go off the rails. Compared to drugs and gambling, an obsession with sex of any kind is a lesser evil providing, of course, that no-one else gets hurt in the process. I have never had a problem with consenting adults in any way, shape or form. So long as they know what they are doing and keep quiet about it, they can get on and do whatever they like. I neither need, nor want to be told and I don't like it rammed down my throat. If you'll pardon the expression.

The key, however, is the word 'adult'. When their excesses and perversions extend to those more fragile and vulnerable than themselves – children being the obvious but not only example – then it's a different matter.

Our society is nowhere near ready for them yet, if, indeed, it ever will be. For the time being, such people have to take responsibility for their behaviour or learn to suppress their inclinations. If they are victims of their own upbringings or past experiences then, I'm sorry, but for thousands of years society has rooted out such people and, by and large, ostracised them. For good reason. The price of allowing them free reign is simply too high.

Except, of course, when society becomes too tolerant, too corrupt and too unsure of it's own values.

Which takes us back to the decline of the Roman Empire. Let's hope we don't follow suit.

6000 people die of AIDS in Africa every day

Inter Generational Sex

You soon get to know what people feel passionate about
in the back of a cab. Top of the list are sexual offences
against children. Cabbies I've spoken to would bring back
the death penalty for such offenders without hesitation.
Yet there's an uneasy suspicion that in our increasingly
liberal society things might go the other way.

WE used to call it paedophilia. Not anymore. Who would
have thought that the sexual exploitation of the young and
under-aged could ever be assigned a politically correct
name?

Well it has, and what we will see from now on is the
gradual evolution of paedophiles into a minority group
portraying themselves as hard done by.

Entirely predictable, I suppose, but sadly we shall have
to endure the spectacle of this headline-grabbing, brand-new
minority group – those who cannot control the urge to have
sexual relations with children – applying for 'victim' status.
If they succeed, and they will, then, as with other minority
groups before them, they will become the recipients of
favourable legislation and even lottery and other government
grants, so don't be surprised to see advertisements inviting
applications for "Inter Generational Outreach Workers"
starting to appear in 'The Guardian' and the windows of

your local job centres. Not to mention government sponsored self-help and counselling groups.

The media will love it. Picture the headlines – "Can Sex Between Consenting Adults and Minors be Beneficial in a Loving Relationship?" followed by 'real-life' case histories of young adults whose lives were improved beyond measure as a result of a loving, sexual relationship with a step-father or 'guardian'.

If you think this is sick, think back less than half a century. The acceptance of homosexuals into the mainstream of society such as we have today, for example, would have been unthinkable then, as would the politics of positive discrimination in general. Putting aside the rights and wrongs of this trend towards extreme tolerance, we have no choice but to acknowledge its power across all political persuasions.

The brand of liberal thinking which prevails in some, thankfully not all, corridors of Whitehall, town halls and local authorities, began in the 60's along with flower-power, ban the bomb and free love. It was based on the premise that if you let people do what Nature dictates, the whole of society will progress to a state of peaceful unselfishness, as so aptly portrayed by the Beatles in their 60's anthem 'All You Need is Love'. These naïve ideas were rightly abandoned in the seventies and eighties, surviving only in a few key policy making areas such as education, welfare and social services. Seemingly overnight, in a society where nearly two generations had never experienced war or severe hardship, the principle of every individual being held responsible for his or her actions was turned on its head and replaced by the 'victim' culture. In other words, the culture of 'it's not my fault'.

Politicians quickly saw the mileage of jumping on to this new bandwagon, spotting that, in an outdated political system where no party had a real hook on which to hang it's hat, this new 'victim culture' could provide rich pickings. Deprived of the class system with its divides and chasms on which to build opposing political positions – and reluctant to deal with the real issues of the day such as immigration, the multicultural society and drugs - politicians realised that here was an opportunity to win an entirely new kind of vote whilst, at the same time, portraying themselves as modern, progressive, compassionate and caring.

Along with this came the realisation that if the country was no longer divided neatly into bosses and workers, the electorate would have to be broken down into smaller and smaller groups, each of which could be 'targeted', and all of which together added up to a majority. This is how New Labour, itself a sham and little more than the old Labour Party led by a Conservative leader, got into power in the first place. Paraphrasing Churchill only slightly, Tony Blair, Peter Mandelson and Alastair Campbell did not accept that 'you can't appeal to all of the people all of the time'. As we've seen, however, delivery (as they call it) is quite another matter.

Hence the 60's liberalists lived to see their dreams come true, not for the reasons they'd expected but because it suited a new breed of politicians to high-jack their childish ideas and re-package them as the new, caring, compassionate society. In the process any minority representing itself as repressed, under-resourced or simply unnoticed, acquired considerable clout in the community.

Ever wondered why the views of the sleeping majority go unheeded? Now you know.

I'll accept that I may have overstated the point about paedophilia to deal with the wider issue. Actually, I confess to knowing little about the subject and, following the experiences of a friend, I'm reluctant to try to find out. In the course of conducting some research for a television programme dealing with child pornography, he visited a number of websites and received an e-mail from the FBI telling him he was engaged in an illegal activity! Not easy, then, to mug up on this particular hot potato.

Watch this space.

A man who kidnapped and sexually assaulted a three-year-old girl was sentenced to 'life imprisonment' of eighteen years. The judge said that under existing rules he could expect to be free on parole after five years and four months.

The Queen

*Black cabs may not be a breeding ground for republicans
but you'll hear many an exasperated remark from behind
the wheel at the latest gaffes of Charles, Camilla, Andrew,
Fergie, Wills, Harry, Phil or even Good Queen Bess
herself. If only she could get the family act together...*

I feel sorry for her, I really do.

She can't be promoted or demoted, can't resign, and clearly doesn't feel inclined to retire. No faith in her son and heir, presumably. Or, she's trying to break some record or another, like Tiger Woods is trying to out-do Jack Nicklaus by winning more majors. Either way, she's got nowhere to go unless, of course, we fire her.

The irony is if we did – and there are some who would like to – she'd still be Queen of England. Certainly, we could make her life more difficult, take away a large chunk of her income, the bit that isn't hers, or force her to live in more modest circumstances, but she'd still be Queen of England. Charles and William would still be future Kings. It's entirely a matter of how we treat them.

Europe, indeed the world, is full of deposed monarchs. They get on with their lives despite what their ex-subjects think and however the pendulum of public opinion swings for or against them. Even the great dictator Franco changed his mind when he realised he couldn't stay in power forever. He re-introduced the Spaniards to their Royal family and they've enjoyed a love affair ever since.

So, love them or hate them, the truth is we can't get rid of them for the simple reason we already did. When King John signed the Magna Carta in 1215 he began the process of handing over power from the Monarch to the people. What he didn't give away was remedied four centuries later with the Bill of Rights. After that, monarchs no longer retained any real influence over our lives. That should have been the end of the Royal Family and the beginnings of the Republic of Britain. But it wasn't. Since then Kings and Queens, either by example or by sheer force of personality, carried on, oddly with the backing of elected governments, who must have thought they still had a useful role to play. The great ceremonies of state, the honours and the orders, all a sham by republican standards, remained and monarchs continued to 'rule', taking the bouquets in good times and the brickbats when things were bad.

Both Queen Elizabeth (the first) and Queen Victoria gave their names to long and prosperous periods in our history when this little island of ours considered itself to be 'on top of the world'. What did they have to do with these great victories and achievements? Probably very little. In fact, Victoria hid herself away for much of her reign in mourning for the German Albert who, ironically, may have done quite a lot.

The reign of our current Queen doesn't bear comparison. If you are going to credit her predecessors with uniting these islands, building an empire, increasing Britain's power and influence in the world, its dominance in trade and commerce then, by the same token, you'd have to say she's lost the lot. She'd also have to own up to the fact she's left little in the way of a legacy, no great buildings, art collections, nothing. In fact, looking back through history, Elizabeth the Second must rank as one of the most benign and ineffectual monarchs of all time.

Not surprising, really. Remember she took over the throne in her early twenties, recalled from her honeymoon in Africa upon the sudden death of her father, himself a reluctant monarch, and flown back to be met by Churchill and the Queen Mother, probably the two most popular and experienced public figures of their time. Between them, or so it must have seemed, they had just won the war. Imagine what they would have said when the gorgeous young newly wed descended the steps of her plane: "Don't worry your pretty little head, dear, leave everything to us", or words to that effect. And she did.

Could things have turned out differently?

Yes, I think so. You can take the power out of the job, but not out of the person. Who's to say that had heredity dealt another hand, we might have had a different kind of monarch, one with more resolve, more determination, far less inclined simply to keep his or her back to the wall?

That's not to say she isn't a very nice lady, probably too nice. Perhaps, even, a bit too normal. She's never looked comfortable with all that pomp and frippery. In fact, I've often wondered whether she wouldn't have been happier lolling around in a quilted dressing gown, with a take-away in front of "Eastenders".

It might have helped if she'd managed to spawn a less dysfunctional family, but then it could be said that in this day and age that's pretty normal, too.

So, what do we do with a more-or-less normal, elderly lady, mother to a normal kind of family who is token head of what has become a rather unexceptional country?

Well, normally in such a situation we'd do nothing. Which is, I suspect, despite the occasional token flurry of republicanism, exactly what we will do.

Probably a good result taking all things into account.

"Modern royalty is in the 'happiness business'."

MARTIN CHARTERIS, THE QUEEN'S FAVOURITE PRIVATE SECRETARY

The Moral Maze

*What follows is a brave attempt to sum up a whole
range of philosophical and ethical points, which
have arisen too often to count during my various
journeys to and fro across the metropolis.*

SOUNDS old-fashioned, doesn't it? Yet, it is the most important puzzle of all - if we can get to grips with it.

What are morals and do they have any place in modern-day life? Well, you certainly don't hear as much about them as you used to.

Mind you, many words that used to be commonplace now sound out-of-date. Words like 'bravery', 'courage', 'duty', 'honour' and 'loyalty' were once the beacons by which people navigated their whole lives. Now these words are virtually extinct and 'morality' is fast finding its way to the front of the same queue.

Fortunately, morals won't go down without a fight. We can rake them over, revise them, freshen them up even, but they will always be there in one form or another. Nevertheless, they are starting to look less resilient than they used to.

Can morals be different for different people? Is it possible that a terrorist who straps a bomb to his body and kills dozens of people, including himself, is behaving morally? Yes - and no. That's the trouble with morals. If he were to behave like that in peacetime, certainly not, but if his people were at war then, yes, he would be behaving no differently to the soldiers on the other side. So, then, do soldiers behave morally? Well, throughout history we have assumed that it is moral to kill the enemy in pursuit of the greater good. However, take the war in Iraq and you will find opinion sharply divided and I don't mean just between those of differing cultural and religious backgrounds, I mean amongst any group of people you choose to ask.

Is it possible that morals can change with the times? It would seem so. When I was a teenager it was regarded as immoral to sleep with your partner before marriage. Today, only a quarter of a century later, such a view would seem absurd. In fact, dozens of pursuits we consider perfectly acceptable today were widely thought to be immoral less than a lifetime ago: sex before marriage, contraception, homosexuality, masturbation, pornography, blasphemy, swearing, lying, euthanasia, even alcohol and recreational drugs, to name but a few.

What are we left with? Well, for the time being we still consider theft and violence to be immoral, definitely sex with children and possibly (but only just) adultery. We've already excluded killing under the heading of 'war' and I suppose we have to omit lying and deceit simply because they are now so widely practised by politicians and the media. Yesterday's moral lapses have become today's tools of the trade.

We're not talking about minimal shifts in perception either, but total reversals. Homosexual behaviour, for example, not long ago punishable by law, is now promoted in schools by Act of Parliament and protected by new legislation pronouncing the exact opposite!

How can we take morals seriously when this kind of turnaround can happen? Where are our points of reference?

In a shifting world where we seem to be able to adapt moral values to suit convenience, is it worth worrying about morals at all? What are they, anyway, if not merely signposts along the highways and byways of day-to-day behaviour? Do they matter, or are they just a hangover from another age when the Church cradled us in the palm of its hand and taught us the Ten Commandments?

Or, were they only ever a device used by rulers and bishops to curb our more base and animal instincts in the interests of building a co-operative and well-behaved society?

One thing is sure. Getting people to live by some sort of moral code is a lot easier and cheaper than relying on the law. So it's not surprising that, at a time when our moral consensus is at an all time low, we are burdened by more and more legislation and overflowing prisons.

It also seems pretty clear that when a gang of 'hoodies' is brought before the court for GBH, its members have no idea they have done anything wrong. Who, in truth, can blame them? These are not kids who have been brought up in decent Christian homes – if such places still exist – with a clear set of guidelines and firm but fair parenting. These are feral young humans who have been set a sickening example by their parents and are making up the rules as they go along. Sure, we can punish them but, eventually, they will find themselves back amongst us with no better understanding of what's right and wrong than before.

Take another example. If you tell me that I have to pay for insurance to protect against a third party claim before I'm allowed to take to the road, then I understand the sense of that and I'm happy to comply. Elsewhere, South Africa for example, they include the cost of third party insurance in the price of the petrol. Why? Because they know they haven't a hope in hell of convincing two thirds of the population to pay in advance. Tell me, where do morals come in to that? The answer is they don't. It's a different way of seeing things. In our new multi-cultural society, if we expect everyone to think the same and try to enforce an out-dated moral code by law, the prison service will get so overloaded we'll have no choice but to repeatedly shorten sentences to the extent that imprisonment will cease to act as a deterrent.

So, there's the reality. Where do we go from there?

Since moral dilemmas crop up all the time we need to get a handle on them and fast. It's no good having one set of rules for one section of society and a different set for another. Take the police and drugs. How can we possibly justify tolerance towards one ethnic group whilst prosecuting another? This is discrimination and the fact that it 'favours' the minority merely results in an open invitation to the majority to break the law.

In fact, it could be argued with good reason that any form of discrimination is intrinsically immoral. If so, a great deal of so-called 'positive' discrimination favouring minorities is fundamentally wrong.

Of course, we must not confuse immorality with evil. I know one or two thoroughly immoral people who manage to live their lives without causing any great harm or inconvenience to others. They may be misguided but that's another thing. Read on.

When George and Yo-Blair decided to invade Iraq, how much consideration did they give to the moral issues involved? Conveniently, they are both self-proclaimed Christians and the Bible does say 'an eye for an eye and a tooth for a tooth' thus paving the way for doing pretty much anything you fancy to anyone you don't like.

The really surprising thing about Iraq was that there appeared to be little if any moral debate at all. Even the

UN couldn't make up its mind when the moral argument was so one-sided as to be staring them in the face. Tell me, with the benefit of hindsight, can you see what possible moral justification there could have been to launch a full-scale military attack on Iraq? But, when the chips were down, the moral argument carried little weight. It would seem that modern, industrial warfare is immune to questions of morality.

Throughout history our leaders have been faced with difficult decisions, hopefully decisions which you and I will never have to make, most of them falling into the category of 'the end justifying the means.' Within the context of everyday life I have no doubt that doing something bad in order to avoid something worse is a mistake. If only because the only thing you can be sure of is that you are doing something bad. What happens after that can only be guessed at.

The hardest military decisions fall into this category: whether to sacrifice the lives of the few in order to save the lives of many. That's hard to stomach and I'd like to know whether any historical analysis has proved in retrospect how many such decisions have been justified in the light of subsequent events. What does the moralist have to say? Precious little it would seem. Even now that the folly of Iraq is apparent, there is still a reluctance to wholeheartedly condemn those who led us into such an immoral conflict. Conviction on such issues is in short supply.

At the end of the day morality is either consistent, robust and universal or it isn't worth a light. When it becomes elastic, to be stretched and distorted in all directions to suit the mood of the moment, then it ceases to have any value. When you say that 'young people have no morals nowadays' you are wrong. It's just that their morals are not the same as yours.

So, like just about everything else in our divided and increasingly diverse society, the old morality is fragmenting before our eyes. And yet, as daily life becomes increasingly confusing and complicated, we need moral and ethical guidelines more than ever.

Maybe we are getting to the stage when we have to generate our own moral code from within ourselves rather than having it handed to us on a plate. Fortunately, we all have a conscience and mostly we don't want to go through life feeling guilty and fearful.

In the end, what are morals for if not to help us sleep soundly at night, free from the torment of shame and self-loathing?

Certainly a clear conscience makes it worthwhile devising your own set of rules. But then, of course, that's exactly what the 'hoodies' are doing. How to convince them that their set of rules should conform to ours is another question, and if someone out there knows the answer, I'd like to hear it.

The state can't do it. The moral code we have taken for granted until now was the product of a whole mix of ingredients: a commitment to marriage and the enduring family unit, a set of longstanding Christian values upheld across the whole of society by an active and effective church, a responsible and well-intentioned media and, last but not least, the good example of those in positions of authority - plus, in order for it all to work, an acceptance that each and every individual is responsible for his or her own actions. The very things we now seem intent upon systematically destroying.

It can take centuries to painstakingly build something of value but only days to dismantle it. If you have to knock something down in order to rebuild it, then you need to know what you're going to put in its place before you start.

It is unrealistic to think that by chucking yesterday's moral code on the bonfire, a new one will rise like a Phoenix from the ashes.

"There's a moral vacuum in Britain - and if we don't return to our Christian values, we may not be able to resist Islam."

MICHAEL NAZIR-ALI, BISHOP OF ROCHESTER

Tiger for President!

*Someone once said the most important thing you need
to get through life is a sense of humour. Somebody
else said many a true word is spoken in jest.*

IF this weren't such a good idea it would be laughable.

We've had Ronald Reagan, a b-movie actor, and Arnold
Schwarzenegger, an a-movie actor, both rising to the pinnacle
of American politics. So, what's to stop the greatest golfer in
the world becoming President?

Listen, surely by the time he's forty he's going to be
wondering what to do next. By then he'll be astonishingly
wealthy – not for him the worries of paying the mortgage or
school fees – and a bit bored.

He's already famous all over the world, and he's multi-
ethnic. Not bad for starters, eh?

On top of this, he's super-intelligent, has a will of iron,
unmatched self-motivation, good looks and charm. Plus, he
scares people without trying. Think what he's achieved in
only a few years, then imagine what he'll be capable of when
he grows up!

When did the world last have a leader who everybody
knew and admired before he got the job? Think about
it. Who had heard of George Bush Jnr before he ran for
President? Contrast that with the appeal of a young man

already at the undisputed top of his field, a proven competitor in a profession which demands impeccable standards of honesty and integrity and where the only way to succeed is through pure merit, year after year after year. And we'd have a President who could really play golf.

Sorry, forget it. It was just an idea.

"Tiger Woods is not only the most fundamentally sound golfer I've ever seen, but an exceptionally composed individual for his years..."

JACK NICKLAUS, 1996 MASTERS

Postscript

HAS it ever occurred to you that when the dinosaurs ruled the world there weren't any humans? Neither was it the dinosaurs, undisputed winners in the great tournament of evolution circa 400 million years ago, who eventually evolved into homo sapiens.

When the dinosaurs finally succumbed to some cataclysmic force of nature (whatever it was and scientists are still arguing) 65m years ago after reigning supreme for 300m years, there was no sign of man at all. We had to wait another 62m years before anything remotely like us appeared, only 3m years ago, in fact. Admittedly, since then, we've steamed ahead like a train.

The point is, where were we in the intervening period? Nowhere to be seen. The seeds of our own creation were contained in some other rather unspectacular form of life, probably lurking under a rock at the bottom of the sea.

Why does this matter, I hear you ask?

Well, let's put it like this: if we didn't announce our intention to take over from the dinosaurs as the most dominant form of life this planet has ever known since Jurassic Park - if, in fact, we weren't even to be spotted above ground - then where are our successors now?

Assuming the likelihood of the earth destroying us rather than the other way round, which is all we ever seem to hear about, then the question must be who will inhabit the planet after we are gone?

It's not particularly original but I think I'd go for ants. After all, they display many of the qualities that seem to have stood us in good stead. They're loyal, industrious, adaptable, gregarious, work in teams, have a well-organised social structure, are good at building large structures, have farms and hospitals and adore their queen. They're also very difficult to destroy.

Of course, they'd have to change a bit over the next few million years. They'd need to get bigger, for one thing. Assuming there will still be some large creatures left in the world, it's difficult to imagine how ants could deal with them in their present size. And they'd need bigger brains, if only to outwit their predators. Other than that, given a fair evolutionary wind, ants seem up for the job.

Alternatively, it could be the turn of a sea creature to take to the tiller. Our ancestors had to make their way ashore for some reason. I can't see why. There's far more sea than land and it's easier to get about. I rather fancy the chances of the octopus. They look clever and crafty with that big head and beady eye housing a mysterious intelligence. Scary, too, which is always helpful if you're out to dominate the world. We won't be there to see it, but it's easy to imagine vast cities on the seabed, patrolled by highly intelligent denizens of the deep safe from the harshness and ravages of life on land.

Or could it be the age of the aviator? Birds and reptiles share common ancestry with us and, depending upon conditions, the ability to fly could just be the deciding factor. After all, where would we be without flight - and we have to rely on mechanical contraptions. Not to mention the fact they don't seem to feel the cold.

At the end of the day (or should it be eon) it will come down to what the world is like in a few million years time. Whether our own species makes it is, at the very least, questionable. If it does, then mankind will have broken all evolutionary records and proved to be the most sustainable and adaptable life form in the history of the earth. Needless to say, if humans survive, they won't be very much like us, nor, probably would we have very much in common. For a start, they almost certainly won't have "Big Brother", not on TV anyway, but then again, they just might.

If we don't make it, then some other species will evolve and it's intriguing to think it's already with us in some shape or form.

So, next time you feed the cat take a closer look at what may be going on behind those big, know-it-all eyes. Clever furry little sods. I wouldn't be surprised.

Coming back to the dinosaurs though, there is a theory that they lost the battle for survival because a 10km wide meteor landed in Mexico and caused a dust cloud which lasted several months or years. Another theory suggests it was that old chestnut climate change that did them in.

Now, just for a moment, imagine that you were in a space station looking at the earth when these things happened. You wouldn't have noticed much - maybe a cloud of dust and a pinprick where the meteor landed. Yet the result was cataclysmic.

The moral, surely, is that life on this planet exists on a knife-edge. It needs only a tiny shift in the balance of things for one life form to be obliterated and to be replaced by another. The earth itself will hardly notice the difference.

If ever we need reminding of the fragility of our existence, and how little we have to do with our own survival, think of the dinosaurs. In their very small brains they must have thought they'd got it made. Nature proved them wrong. It usually does.

The earth may destroy us, it's even possible we may destroy ourselves, but there's one thing you can be sure of - either way Gaia will have the last laugh.

Thank you for reading the book.

"Trying to take on the job of regulating the Earth is about as crazy as you can get."

PROFESSOR JAMES LOVELOCK, INSTITUTE OF
CHEMICAL ENGINEERS, LONDON, NOVEMBER 2006

About the Author

Philip Walsh was born and went to school in Croydon, UK. He has worked as a musician, a graphic designer, in advertising, publishing and television.

He has been married for more than thirty years and has three grown up daughters.

Printed in the United Kingdom
by Lightning Source UK Ltd.
133055UK00001B/20/A